AF594392

Six Drawing Lessons

THE CHARLES ELIOT NORTON LECTURES, 2012

Six Drawing Lessons

WILLIAM KENTRIDGE

Harvard University Press
CAMBRIDGE, MASSACHUSETTS
LONDON, ENGLAND
2014

Printed in Canada

Fourth printing

Publication of this book has been supported through the generous provisions of the Maurice and Lula Bradley Smith Memorial Fund.

Book design by Dean Bornstein

Library of Congress Cataloging-in-Publication Data

Kentridge, William, 1955–
[Works. Selections]
Six drawing lessons / William Kentridge.
pages cm. — (The Charles Eliot Norton lectures)
ISBN 978-0-674-36580-3 (alk. paper)
1. Art. 2. Aesthetics. I. Title.
N7396.K45A35 2014
701—dc23

2013047425

For Alice, Isabella, and Samuel

CONTENTS

1 In Praise of Shadows 1

2 A Brief History of Colonial Revolts 33

3 Vertical Thinking: A Johannesburg Biography 69

4 Practical Epistemology: Life in the Studio 99

5 In Praise of Mistranslation 129

6 Anti-Entropy 157

Six Drawing Lessons

Drawing Lesson One

IN PRAISE OF SHADOWS

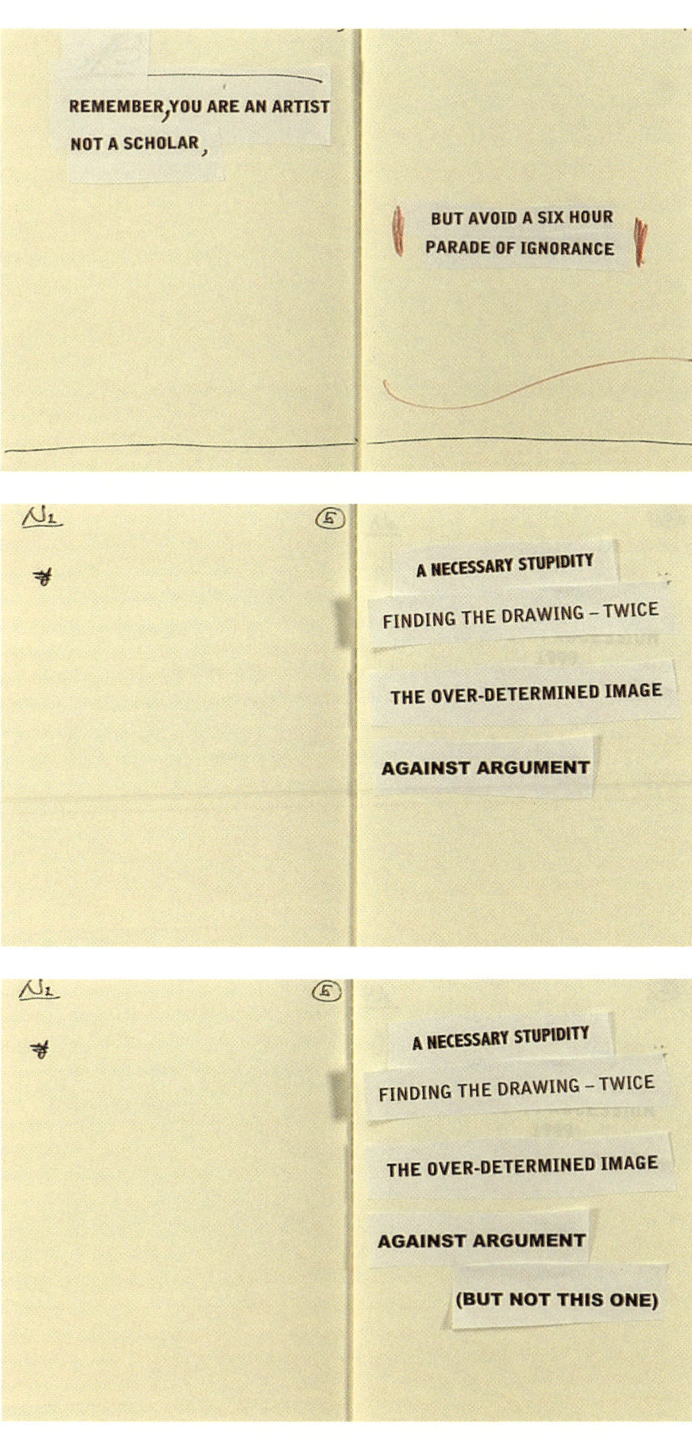
REMEMBER, YOU ARE AN ARTIST
NOT A SCHOLAR,
BUT AVOID A SIX HOUR
PARADE OF IGNORANCE
A NECESSARY STUPIDITY
FINDING THE DRAWING – TWICE
THE OVER-DETERMINED IMAGE
AGAINST ARGUMENT
A NECESSARY STUPIDITY
FINDING THE DRAWING – TWICE
THE OVER-DETERMINED IMAGE
AGAINST ARGUMENT
(BUT NOT THIS ONE)

IN PRAISE OF SHADOWS

ABOUT ten months ago, I telephoned my father to say that I had been invited to deliver this series of lectures.

"Well," he replied, "do you have anything to say?"

"But you understand it is a great honor to be asked to give the Norton Lectures."

"Indeed," he said, "and now you have that honor. You don't have to accept."

But it seems the decision has been made, and here we are, and the six lectures that follow will be an attempt to answer that first question.

On the first day I started thinking about the lectures, I made a note, a caution to myself, which I repeat today:

REMEMBER YOU ARE AN ARTIST, NOT A SCHOLAR.
BUT AVOID A SIX-HOUR PARADE OF IGNORANCE.

Notes like this one are an essential part of the preparation process. I listed every thought I had ever had, or remembered someone else's having. I divided them by six—in many different ways, as if in their different arrangements some new thought would emerge. I wrote them on pieces of paper and pinned them to the walls of the studio.

A NECESSARY STUPIDITY
FINDING THE DRAWING TWICE
THE OVER-DETERMINED IMAGE
AGAINST ARGUMENT

AGAINST CERTAINTY
GEOLOGICAL AUTOCHTHONY

I added them to drawings I was making.

AGAINST ARGUMENT (BUT NOT THIS ONE)
A UNIVERSAL ARCHIVE
KNOWLEDGE AS SHAME
LESSONS FROM TYPEWRITERS
DIALECTICS FOR NINE-YEAR-OLDS
IN PRAISE OF BASTARDY
A HISTORY OF CINEMA
A PRE-HISTORY OF RELATIVITY
THE FULL-STOP SWALLOWS THE SENTENCE

I painted them in alizarin crimson watercolor, on pages of a 1735 Franciscan liturgical tract (I was in Rome).

IN PRAISE OF MISTRANSLATION
MEETING THE WORLD HALFWAY
POEMS I USED TO KNOW
MAKING A SAFE SPACE FOR STUPIDITY
DRAWING WITH ONE EYE SHUT
CIRCLING THE STUDIO
PERFORMANCES OF TRANSFORMATION
PICASSO ON SAFARI
VIVA LINOCUT VIVA!
WHAT WE LEARNT AT SUPPER
THE FACE OF THE OTHER (AN ETHICAL DEMAND)
TORSCHLUSSPANIK

Beating into my head the need to find a connection between the activity I practiced, drawing, and the words of the lecture.

At the beginning, let it be said that these lectures will move forward and backward through the studio. I hope they are more

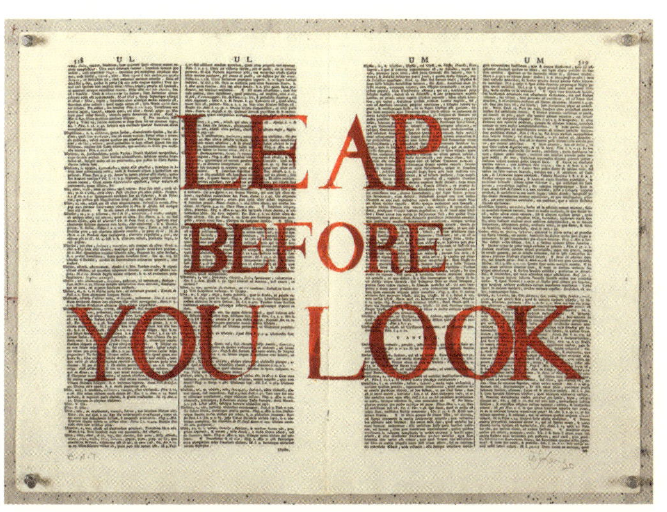
LEAP
BEFORE
YOU LOOK

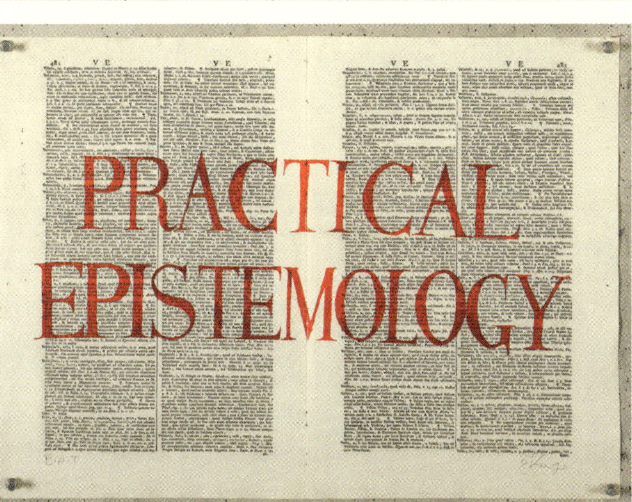
PRACTICAL
EPISTEMOLOGY

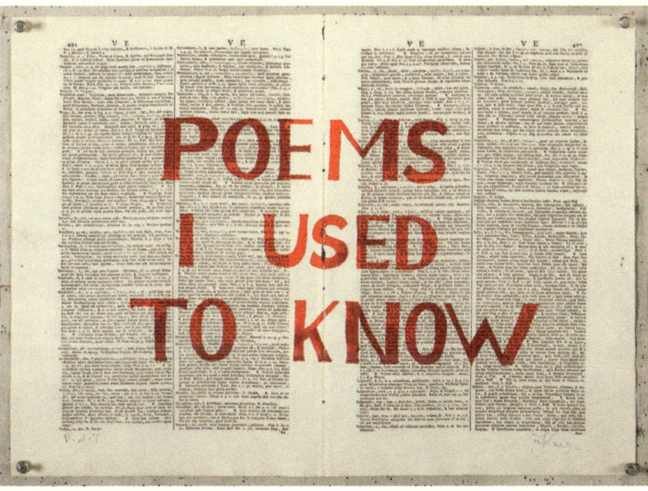
POEMS
I USED
TO KNOW

than a description of the work I have done over the last thirty years, but to start away from that would be folly.

This is about a necessary movement from image to idea. We will start each lecture either with a short film or with an extract from a larger piece of work I have made, both to show the images I am thinking about when talking, or to which the lectures refer, but also, and importantly, to state the primacy of the image and the making of the image, in the thinking behind the construction of the lecture. This primacy is literal. The works I will show sometimes come from a decade ago, and the thinking about them sometimes six months ago.

We start today with a part of a film made thirteen years ago. The section I will show is approximately five minutes long.

[Show film clip from *Shadow Procession.*]

Let us begin in 360 BCE. Here is Plato, writing in the voice of Socrates, in his book *The Republic:*

> "Imagine an underground chamber like a cave, with a long entrance open to the daylight and as wide as the cave. In this chamber are men who have been prisoners there since they were children, their legs and necks being so fastened that they can only look straight ahead of them and cannot turn their heads. Some way off, behind and higher up, a fire is burning, and between the fire and the prisoners and above them runs a road, in front of which a curtain-wall has been built, like the screen at puppet shows between the operators and their audience, above which they show their puppets."

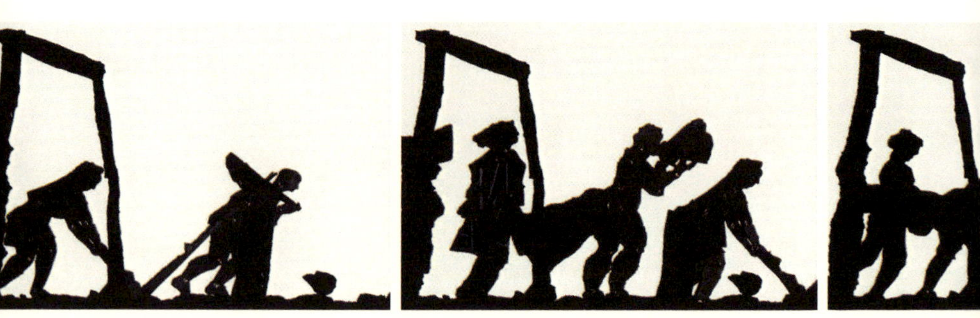

> "I see."
>
> "Imagine further that there are men carrying all sorts of gear along behind the curtain-wall, projecting above it and including figures of men and animals made of wood and stone and all sorts of other materials, and that some of these men, as you would expect, are talking and some not."
>
> "An odd picture and an odd sort of prisoner."

This text, which is worth reading in its extended form, is not just the center point for this lecture, but also the starting point for a line we will follow through the series of lectures. The questions it provokes, its metaphors, are the pivotal axes of questions both political and aesthetic. However, at this point, let us simply note the presence of prisoners in the story.

> "They are drawn from life," I replied. "For, tell me, do you think our prisoners could see anything of themselves or their fellows except the shadows thrown by the fire on the wall of the cave opposite them?"
>
> "How could they have seen anything else if they were prevented from moving their head all their lives?"
>
> "And would they see anything more of the objects carried along the road?"
>
> "Of course not."
>
> "Then if they were able to talk to each other, would they not assume that the shadows they saw were the real things?"
>
> "Inevitably."
>
> "And if the wall of their prison opposite them reflected sound, don't you think that they would suppose, whenever one of the

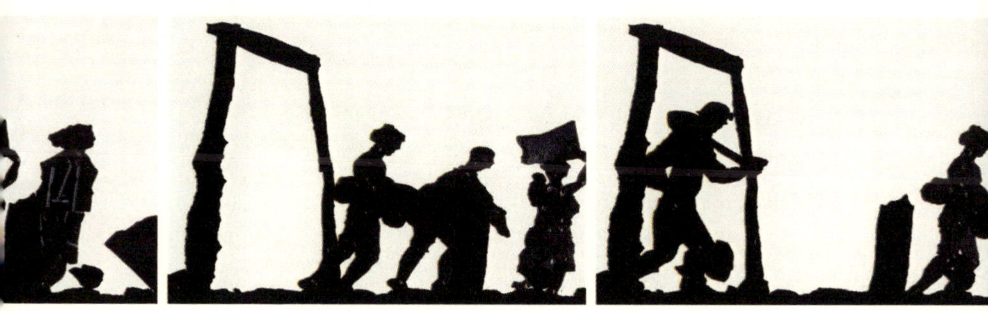

passers-by on the road spoke, that the voice belonged to the shadow passing before them?"

"They would be bound to think so."

Shadow Procession, the film from which I showed an extract at the beginning of this lecture, was made in 1999 for the Istanbul Biennale. It was to be shown in the underground Yerebatan cistern of the city. It uses a technique of jointed paper puppets moved frame by frame under the camera. The torn pieces of paper are joined with twists of wire. Its origins are in puppet theater, in which flat cut-out figures are used either as silhouettes in front of the screen or as shadows cast onto the screen.

"And so in every way they would believe that the shadows of the objects we mentioned were the whole truth."

"Yes, inevitably."

"Then think what would naturally happen to them if they were released from their bonds and cured of their delusions. Suppose one of them were let loose, and suddenly compelled to stand up and turn his head and look and walk towards the fire; all these actions would be painful and he would be too dazzled to see properly the objects of which he used to see the shadows. What do you think he would say if he was told that he was now nearer reality and seeing more correctly, because he was turned towards objects that were more real, and if on top of that he were compelled to say what each of the passing objects was when it was pointed out to him? Don't you think he would be at a loss, and think that what he used to see was far truer than the objects now being pointed out to him?"

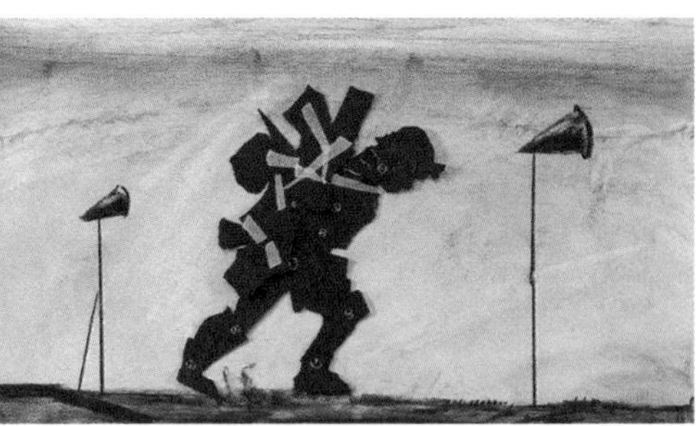

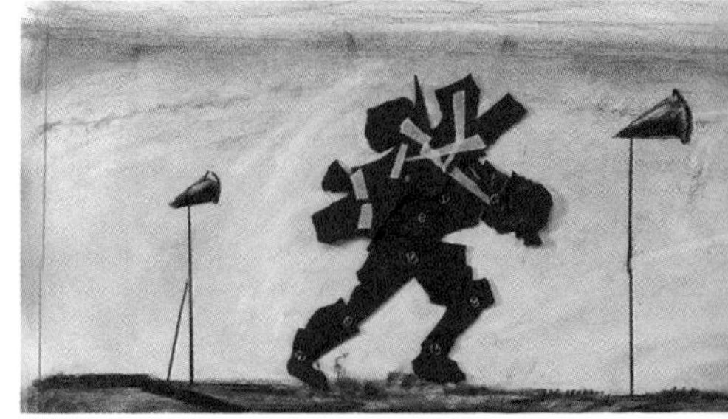

> "Yes, far truer."
>
> "And if he were made to look directly at the light of the fire, it would hurt his eyes and he would turn back and retreat to the things which he could see properly, which he would think really clearer than the things being shown him."

The paper characters in *Shadow Procession* formed on the one hand an inventory of people on the move. A man walking while reading, miners carrying a broken city, pensioners carried in a wheelbarrow. An inventory of specific people seen in newspapers and the news, or on the streets of Johannesburg.

But the film was about amplitude rather than the specific nature of a particular journey. A catalogue of people on the move. I was interested in how roughly a figure could be torn and still be understood; how crudely it could be moved and still have coherence as a moving, specific person.

> "And if," I continued, "he were forcibly dragged up the steep and rugged ascent and not let go till he had been dragged out into the sunlight, the process would be a painful one, to which he would much object, and when he emerged into the light his eyes would be so dazzled by the glare of it that he wouldn't be able to see a single one of the things he was now told were real."
>
> "Certainly not at first," he agreed.

The question of shadows was posed in practical terms. How to achieve an image, not a thought. Shadows and movement. I think my interest in processions started with seeing the Goya image *Procession of the Holy Office and Pilgrimage to San*

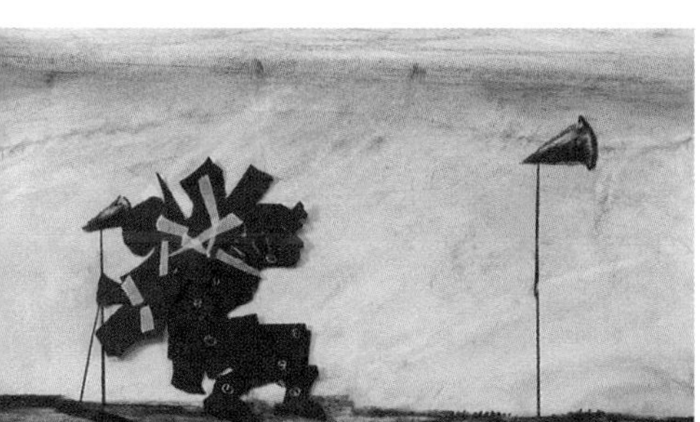

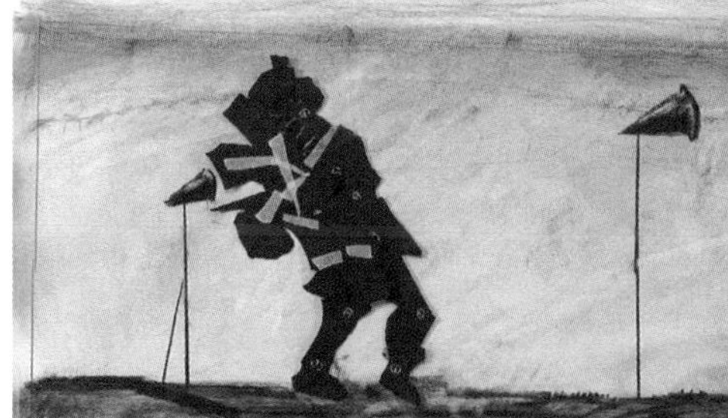

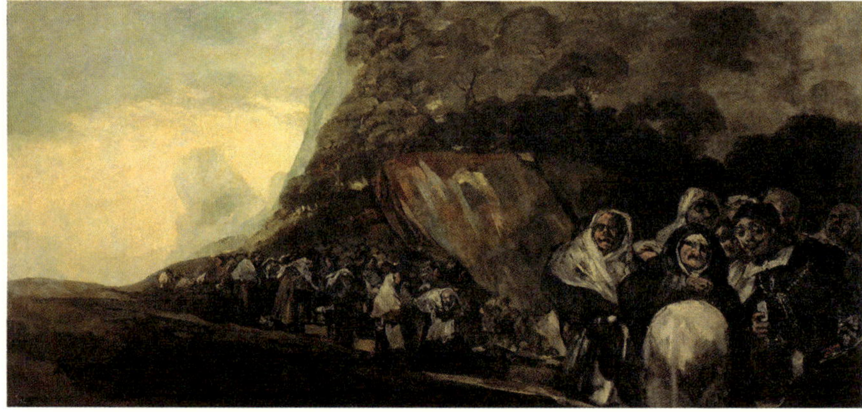

Isidiro—the crowd moving from the depths of the picture plane toward us. With shadows, the forward movement of the image becomes problematic—you have a light source, you have an object blocking the light.

As the crowd moves toward the light source, its shadow gets larger, covering the entire screen or wall, obliterating everything. Its forward flexibility is very limited. Whereas the lateral movement, while reducing a mass to an itemized list, does enable a continuation, a sense of ongoing procession, to be clear. Plato's crowd has of necessity to be a procession, observed neither advancing nor retreating, but passing.

> "Because, of course, he would need to grow accustomed to the light before he could see things in the upper world outside the cave. First he would find it easiest to look at the shadows, next at the reflections of men and other objects in water, and later on at the objects themselves. After that he would find it easier to observe the heavenly bodies and the sky itself at night, and to look at the light of the moon and stars rather than at the sun and its light by day."
>
> "Of course."
>
> "The thing he would be able to do last would be to look directly at the sun itself, and gaze at it without using reflections in water or any other medium, but as it is in itself."
>
> "That must come last."
>
> "Later on he would come to the conclusion that it is the sun that

> produces the changing seasons and years and controls everything in the visible world, and is in a sense responsible for everything that he and his fellow-prisoners used to see."
>
> "That is the conclusion he would obviously reach."

We will come to the question of destination later in the series of lectures. Here, suffice it to say that when making the film, I could not find a destination that felt possible. The procession could not end with a *fête galante* on the island of Cythera of Watteau, nor could it arrive at a civic state, nor at a collective farm. We have reached a point where all destinations, all bright lights, arouse mistrust. The light at the end of the tunnel turns too quickly into the interrogator's spotlight.

> "And when he thought of his first home and what passed for wisdom there, and of his fellow-prisoners, don't you think he would congratulate himself on his good fortune and be sorry for them?"
>
> "Very much so."

From this, Plato tells us, comes the ethical imperative of the philosopher. The man who has seen the light and apprehended the understanding that follows from it has a duty to return to the cave, to unshackle those in darkness, and to bring them up from the cave into the light. If necessary, this must be done with force. The nexus of enlightenment, emancipation, and violence emerges. Our agenda has been set.

IN WORDS ALAS DROWN I

As the medium of these lectures is not charcoal, but talking, perhaps we should pause here for a moment, with some remarks on the discipline itself. There are the words themselves, and their syntax and grammar and their relation to the outside world. But there is also the discipline of the medium, that which is in between the words—the devices which one uses to either pin the words more closely to the world outside or to encourage the listener to make the connection, to convince them of what I say. In Plato we see this clearly, in the form of the rhetorical questions and prompted answers.

> Is it not true that the questions Plato asks have a predicted, prompted answer?
>
> That is quite true.
>
> Are not the questions there to provide a form for moving the argument forward, rather than a real enquiry?
>
> I agree.
>
> And is the argument any weaker for this chosen form of writing?
>
> Inevitably not.
>
> Therefore, must we not say that this mock interrogation is something over and above the words in the sentences that connect to the world—there to convince the reader or listener?
>
> I am bound to think so.
>
> Are not the answers to the questions simply a mode of emphasis, of convincing us?
>
> Yes. Inevitably again. True. Very much so. Necessarily. Yes, that certainly is so. Absolutely true. Something of this sort is inevitable.

But there are many other things that happen in the gaps and spaces, most importantly the . . . the . . . hesitation.

The dramatic um . . . um . . . um . . .

The uncertain UM, the pause before the certainty of the final statement.

Or . . . or . . .

Mock uncertainty, the pause before the clarity of the final statement.

Or . . . or . . .

Mock uncertainty hiding real uncertainty.

And a series of accompanying gestures, unspoken, which are not there in the text (though in truth some of them are here in my notes), but which are an essential part of what the performance, or conversation or talking or lecture, is.

Emphasizing this precise point, the raised finger.

Gathering consensus, while letting thoughts expand, gathering further examples, the circling finger.

The adjustment of the sleeve, the removal of the watch.

A small but important point being made—the thumb and forefinger circle.

The open-handed tapping of the podium.

The collar tug.

The one hand in the pocket.

The double-handed tossing of the salad. The dovening, leaning forward to the notes. The shaking of the dice for emphasis.

A demonstration of other possibilities, the windshield wiper wrist.

The apparent losing of the place in the notes.

The real losing of the place in the notes.

The open-handed, sincere simplicity.

The weighing of words with an open hand.

The removal of the glasses for a frank look. Their replacement. Their almost-replacement, the held gesture.

This complex combination: touching the nose, stroking the hair, the collar tug and the finger twirl, to take us through a complex question.

A separation of the tangential action from the essential thought. The more extreme the action, the purer the thought.

(This catalogue of extra-verbal explanations is derived from a lecture I observed by Mr. Jacques Rancière.)

What is the belief? That from all these words, their grammar, their argument, the conscious or unconscious performance of gestures of conviction—is the belief that from all these truth will be distilled? The belief that all can be stripped bare and evaluated, everything that is designed to hide a false connection can be discovered and discarded. The belief that from the morass surrounding and including the words, we can extract the logical, the justified inference, the truth; and that the rational, the good, the philosopher, the judge will prevail. I am intensely skeptical of such a godlike judge and such judgments, but all the same, I place you, the audience, or the reader, in that position.

PRE-HISTORY OF AN ARTIST

There are many pre-histories to being an artist, how or why one ends up spending one's life filling sheets of paper with signs and images. Some of these we will come across later in the lectures. But suffice it to say that there is obviously a need to arrive at a meaning, without the medium of language and logic—in fact, in opposition to it. A biographical note. I was a high school debater on the school team. We would have formal debates such as: "This House Abhors the Dissolution of the British Empire."

The debates were designed to teach logical argument, rhetorical skill, and to show their importance and value. The reverse happened. It seemed one could equally make an argument for this house abhorring the dissolution of the British Empire, or this house celebrating the dissolution of the British Empire. And in fact one could swap arguments, at ten minutes' notice, if one of the team speakers was missing. Argument and logic became something on top of the world, hovering over its surface, rather than embedded in it. Was something true, or simply convincingly argued? I trusted neither the arguments nor myself.

I think this is also one of the reasons that I did not become an academic—and it should be said here, in this august citadel of scholarship—that I think also I became an artist because I realized I needed a field in which the construction of fictional authorities and imagined quotes would be a cause for celebration, rather than rustication and disgrace.

The thirty years in the studio are an attempt not just to answer the question, "Have you anything to say?" but rather to try to disempower the question. As I indicated at the start of the lecture, the presence of a father who was a lawyer was not incidental to this narrative. It became imperative to make something, a self, impervious to cross-examination. To assert the primacy and the necessity for stupidity, for the necessary stupidity that is essential in the studio. This is a caveat to what follows, which is a series of reflections after the event. Not an interpretation of works I have made, but reflections which stem from them—more specifically, that stem from the activity of making them. There are inevitably interpretations of the work, in which I am situated as a rather privileged, but not particularly skilled, critic. Too close to the person who made them, too subject to his bullying will of how I should see them, to give any helpful advice.

OUR EIGHT-YEAR-OLD SHADOWS

To return to Plato and his myth of shadows, darkness and light—the heart not just of this lecture but of the five lectures that will follow. Let us go back to the cave and the prisoners deceived by the shadows. And I think of an eight-year-old on the beach, and the long shadows cast by the sun close to the horizon. The shadows are a version of you. Lift your arm and the shadow lifts its arm. Step forward and the shadow advances. But the elongation, the anamorphic projection, changes things too. There is a speed, a skill. Ducking and weaving, no one can stand on the shadow. The shadow of the head now up at the dunes at the top of the beach moves twenty meters as I duck down, quick as that. I both control it and delight at a speed and dexterity I did not know that I had. It is an extension and more than an extension of me.

THE PLEASURES OF SELF-DECEPTION

Many years ago, I attended a performance of La Cirque Imaginaire, a miniature circus: an acrobat, his wife, and one untrained goose.

One of the acts of the circus was a performance of the transformation of soap into glass. The performer, the acrobat down from the slack wire, would blow soap bubbles, and then, using a small hammer, would burst each bubble, which had turned to glass. Each glass ball would shatter with the familiar and unmistakable sound of crystal shattering. Every bubble turned to glass as it shattered. The bubbles were glass. Then the performer, with a flick of his wrist, lifted the edge of his waistcoat and showed beneath it a small bell attached to his belt. At the instant he burst each bubble, he tapped the bell, turning the soap into glass. He then blew more bubbles and burst them. Again they turned to glass, even though the bell, the technique, the illusion, was visible. The pleasure changed into the pleasure of being so caught in the pressure of that which could appear and seem, and yet not be.

We the audience became the performers, our act that of believing and disbelieving in the same moment. There is something emerging here, a separation from Plato. The movement of ourselves as more or less enlightened observers toward an awareness of ourselves as agents of understanding. The pleasure in the moment of us believing and not believing at the same time is a jolt of self-assertion. This split, believer and disbeliever, becomes a crack in Plato's edifice.

[Show footage from *Making a Horse.*]

MAKING A HORSE

We take a group of torn black pieces of paper. At first they are a group of black shapes on a white sheet of paper, perhaps with an association to Robert Motherwell. Then we move them about, rearrange them. Now is this about a generosity of viewing, or are we unable to stop ourselves from seeing in them a shape, a form, a horse? Note: this is more than a willing suspension of disbelief in which we know we are seeing torn black sheets of paper but

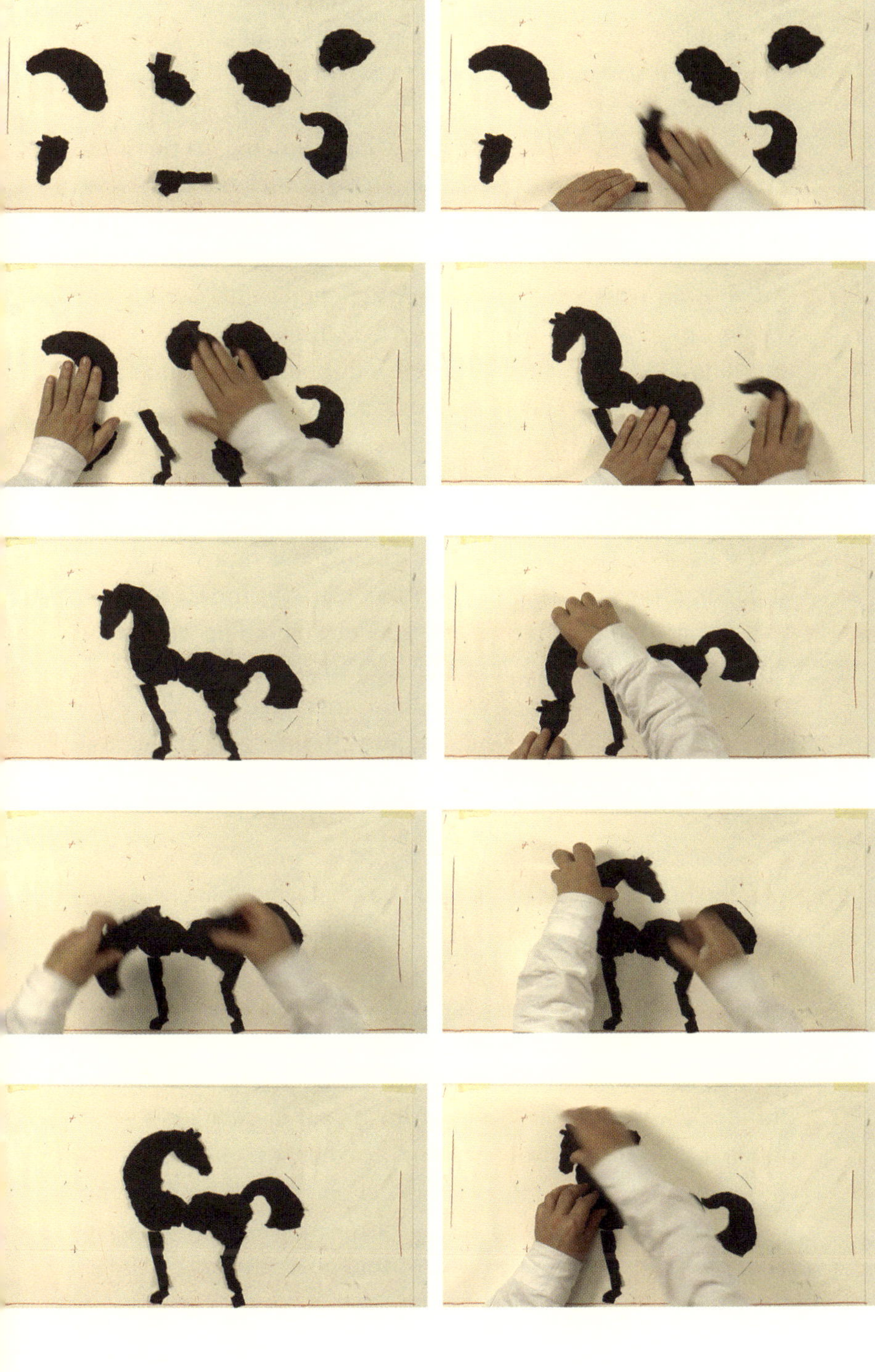

pretend to see a horse. It is much more than that. We cannot help ourselves from seeing the horse. It takes an effort, a willful blindness, to keep the images as black torn sheets of paper. To be more accurate, to see them only as torn sheets of paper. We see them as both, we are not fooled. The horse and the paper are both here. This is an unwilling suspension of disbelief.

When we say there is a horse, we mean there is something on the paper which triggers the recognition of HORSE in us. There is an important distinction here between knowing and recognizing. Ask someone to make a drawing of a horse rearing on its hind legs, and it is not easy (if you are not Delacroix). How far under the rump are the hooves? What is the angle between the mandible and the wing of the atlas? What is the relationship of the withers to the crest and the shoulder of the horse? How much curve in the spine can the belly sustain? What is the articulation of the gaskin to the fetlock? But move the pieces of paper, adjust them, and the horse rears up in front of you. Something we don't know that we know. Something we can recognize without knowing.

This pressure for meaning, taking the fragments and completing an image, is present not only in this looking at shadows but in all that we see. Seeing here becomes a metaphor for all the images, and all the ways we apprehend the world.

Even as the shapes are reduced and the image simplifies, we have the horse with us. Even as it is a single glyph, we will see a horse in its fragments and reconstruct a Rocinante from them.

Inside, there is a sense of HORSE, of horse-ness, waiting to be triggered. Rocinante, Bucephalus, the Trojan horse, Stubbs, the photo-finish in a horse race, are all there. This is a dual process. The sheet of paper comes toward us, and our own sense of horse goes out to it. We meet the world halfway. The sheet of paper with its black shapes on it has become the membrane through which we meet the world. This is both obvious and surprising. The drawing becomes a meeting point, but also a threshold where the outside world meets us—where it meets the Stubbs, Rocinante, encyclopedia entries, memories of horse-riding, memories of falling off a horse and being dragged, foot in stirrup, along the ninth fairway of a golf course, in the Sani Pass holiday resort, at ten years of age.

In some silent invisible vestibule of the brain, the images are caught, apprehended, interrogated, and sent, brushed up, to the resting place as a horse. The sheet of paper is simply a visible extension of the retina, an emblematic demonstration of that which we know but cannot see. Our projection, our moving out toward the image, is an essential part of what it is to see, to be in the world with our eyes open.

To bring this back to Plato's cave: the recognition of the shapes on the wall is not a mistake, an aberration of people caught by illusion, but an essential part of how all parts of the world are apprehended and comprehended.

MEMBRANE OF PAPER

All drawing works with the precept of the paper as the membrane between us and the world. In one extreme case, like a *trompe l'oeil*, the membrane becomes almost invisible, and we think we see the world directly—the book, the playing card—not its artificial recreation. Although in most cases, the pleasure of the *trompe l'oeil* is that of being tricked and not tricked at the same time, the pleasure of our own self-deception, our awareness of the double game, which has become a triple game: the book and playing card we know, the awareness of the paint, oil, glaze, and canvas which makes the illusion of the book and card, and thinking of ourselves, our self-awareness of looking.

The other end of the scale from the *trompe l'oeil* is a system of divination which exists in the north of South Africa and, I am told, along the east coast of Africa. Instead of all the clues to meaning of the image being given on the cloth, or the canvas—the shape, the shadows, the form—all is blank. A Robert Ryman of possibilities. A white cloth is suspended on a wall in a dim room. With the help of a diviner, the client or subject sees into the cloth, seeing images on it of the future, of enemies—all is projection from the eyes outward.

We traverse the difficult space between "I dreamt" and "there came to me in a dream." We as projectors or receivers of that which is in us, that we don't know; or as recipients and transmitters of the world outside.

A BLIND IMPULSE

This seeing into the blank sheet feels familiar to me.

[Film starts.]

The blank sheet of paper awaiting its marks. It is not that a drawing superimposes itself on the surface. But there is an urge, an impulse to make the mark. Possible marks or shapes, projected out onto the paper. A diagonal starting here, leading to an edge here. A line here, or lowered to this point. The shape we will find only when we start to draw—a mixture of making and looking.

Perhaps this is a good place to talk about the division between making and looking, between the ARTIST AS MAKER and the ARTIST AS VIEWER. This is a very real division.

[Show film sequence of *Drawing a Rhinoceros.*]

WK 1 draws a rhinoceros.
Enter WK 2. Observes WK 1. Offers advice.

WK 2: The legs are too squat. The belly needs more heft.

WK 1: Pauses. Looks at WK 2. Continues drawing.

WK 2: The shoulder looks dislocated. Draw better. More application. For god's sake, that tail!

Exit WK 2.

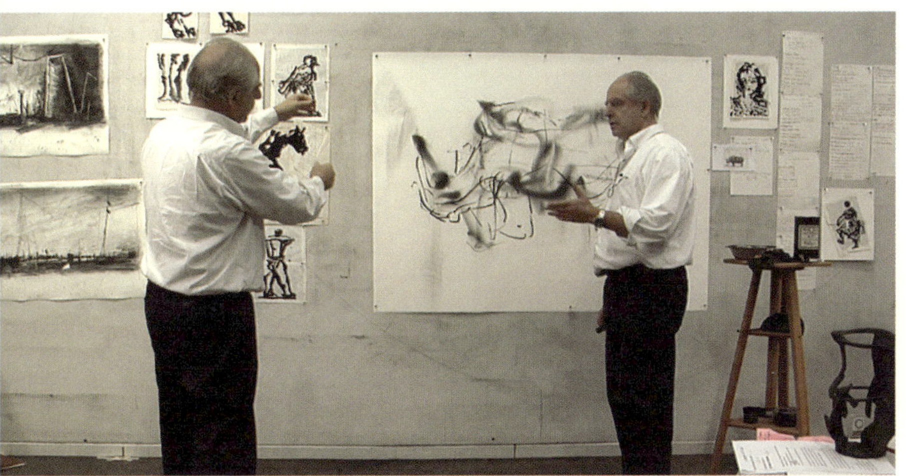

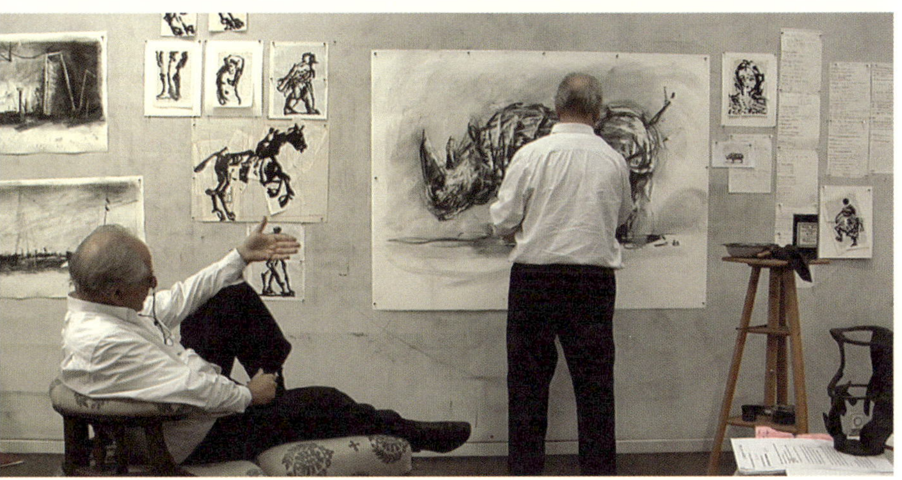

WK 1 reapplies himself to the drawing.

Enter WK 2.

WK 2: Here, look. In the book, it shows how it should be done. Look at how Dürer does this.

WK 1: I am not ready for you.

WK 2: Just look at these very excellent photographs.

WK 1: Could you just leave.

Raised voices, altercation between WK 1 and WK 2.
WK 2 exits.
WK 1 draws furiously—

WK 2 reclines on a chaise longue. Observes WK 1.
WK 1 continues drawing rhinoceros.

I feel here like the artist as viewer, a spokesman. I have the artist as maker looking over my shoulder, checking what I say, kicking my shins when the reflections and projections get too far from the studio—which will be often. And I will try to allow talking to have the same openness as the smooth clean paper awaiting its deformation. As if this talking could be like drawing, taking us from what we know to an image, a site, an insight we did not know we knew. Making a space for uncertainty. Making a safe space for uncertainty. This is in the notes I wrote:

STUDIO AS NUCLEAR-FREE ZONE.
HERE THERE IS A PAUSE
It says, HERE THERE IS A PAUSE, in the notes.

A separation between me writing, in my notebook, and the self walking around the studio thinking, how can we continue?

LOOKING AT THE SUN

To return to Plato and looking at the sun: Of course Plato is talking metaphorically, but perhaps a literal examination is productive in examining the metaphor. What is this light shed by the sun we take for granted, the even brightness on a wall? The sun itself is of course too bright to look at directly. Plato's philosophers would all have been blinded.

CONCERNING AN ECLIPSE

Some years ago, there was a partial eclipse of the sun in Johannesburg. Being well versed in the dangers of looking at the sun directly, I made a hole with a pin in a sheet of paper and looked at the tiny speck of light let through this hole forming a bright circle on a sheet of paper held below. And saw the shadow of the moon move across the circle of light—a minute crescent of darkness eating into the disk of the sun. The daylight receded, and there was a thick dusk on us. I went inside.

In the front room of my house is a window obscured by creepers. The sun shines through the gaps in the foliage, with a pattern of sunlight thrown on the floor, between the shadows of the leaves. The front room was filled with a gloom I expected. But what I had not expected, and what astonished me, was to see in the spots of light on the floor, of the sun between the shadows of the leaves, not just a darkening, but in each one, a crescent eating into the light. Sixty-five patches of light on the floor, sixty-five different-sized crescents, eating into each area of light. There were as many moons as places where sunlight fell. Divide the spaces in half, the moons doubled. A thousand spots of light, a thousand moons and suns.

Again, in retrospect, this is obvious. Every pinhole of all the thousands of people in the city looking at the eclipse had its own shadow of the moon. But more than that, it meant that every pinhole had its own sun. The gaps between the leaves, each one an image not just of the shadow of the moon, but a projection of the sun as well. The sun projects its own image. What I had taken to be light, a generally diffused brightness, was an enormous and infinite series of specific projections, projections of the sun, which turn into an even light as the specific images overlap, multiply, and so blur, to become the even light on the wall.

There is an important inversion here. It is not a case of thousands of eyes looking at an object—we all look at the tree and see it. But it is also the tree projecting itself again and again, directed at you, now you, now you. AN ENDLESS PROMISCUITY OF PROJECTIONS. The studio filled with projections of each table, of each drawing pinned up on the wall, saturated with them. Turn this way, and the images fly in. Every corner of the studio suffused with images waiting to enter.

THE UNIVERSAL ARCHIVE

In the mid-nineteenth century, attempts were made to fix the speed of light. Using mirrors, prisms, spinning disks, it was found that light traveled not infinitely fast, but at an invariant speed of approximately 186,000 miles per second. Light and a projection take a finite time to get from site of generation to site of reception.

Expanding from this discovery, the German scientist Felix Eberty postulated all of space as a universal archive of all that had happened on earth. The light of every event was moving out from the earth at a speed of 186,000 miles per second. If one was at the right point in space, one could see any event that had happened. Near a star 2,000 light years away, one could see Pontius Pilate washing his hands, as Eberty wrote. Near a star 500 years away, Luther could be seen nailing his 95 theses up on the church door at Wittenburg. Felix Eberty took all his examples from the scriptures. His father, one Abraham Ephraim, had converted from Judaism to Lutheranism.

Every action, heroic or shameful, was there to be seen. Every secret deed was visible. There is something terrifying in this. Once launched, an image, an event, a discus, cannot be called back. It has the pressure of perfect memory. It has the same inevitability as the claim that no keystroke is ever lost, that once done, something cannot be undone. The email cannot be unsent. Every foolishness is there, every embarrassment. The universal archive becomes also an overstocked, miserable collection of surplus images. We are caught between wanting to send ourselves out and to hold back, to call back, to annul and obliterate so many traces and acts.

TO UNDO.
TO UNSAY.
TO UNREMEMBER.
TO UNHAPPEN.

The air is thick with images—time made dense with each event and its image, a soup, a fog, as if one could take a sheet of paper and swing it through the air, catching the images as they crashed into it. A swing of the arm above our head to catch the images from us, moving outward, or a low pass to catch those images coming in. On the one, images of the studio, table, charcoal, half-finished drawings, the hand writing these notes, the ideas half formed, the clarity I had two minutes ago, now gone. On the sheet above my head, the trees outside the window, the city beyond that, the traffic, the news, yesterday's news, the strikes, riots, distress in different corners of the world. The porous membrane.

Let us see where we are. Both receiving all the projections that come toward us, listening, a receiving station, scanning the earth for reports of the world, bombarded by particles of information we cannot escape. And transmitting, projecting, broadcasting ourselves continually. Here I am. HERE I AM. Here I am. And between the two, the receiving station and the transmitting station, all our private engines of making sense of the world.

The image of the sheltering paper catching the radiation as it reaches us, or containing an ever-proliferating self, is of course an over-dramatization. But what it does indicate or refer to is the need to push this process of making sense outside, beyond one's own boundaries, onto the drawing, the film, the essay, to find the mediated space between "it is" and "it seems to me."

ALL POWER TO THE . . .

Plato's allegory of the cave was part of a larger project for constructing a vision of an ideal state, an ideal republic, and a philosopher-king who would preside over it. The relationship of knowledge to power is central to Plato. The apprehension of the forms, the move from shadows to light, is what one remembers of the myth, but there is more to be seen in the cave. The philosopher who had seen the light, the sun, apprehended the forms, reached an understanding of the world, had the responsibility of returning to the cave, undoing the shackles and chains of those watching the wall, and bringing them, by force, up to the light.

There are several later associations to this image of those locked in the darkness of the cave. For remember, the people in the cave—not just incidentally, but centrally, for the allegory to work—are chained neck and feet, so they can only see forward to the shadows. They have been like this since childhood. The shackles are more than medieval stocks, in which the prisoner becomes the object of the gaze of others rather than someone looking himself.

But with the insistence of the restriction of the head movement, we are reminded of the yoke and fetters of slaves—a double image: the yokes and fetters of slaves as they are marched across Africa to the slave markets; but more especially, fettered inside the darkness of the hulls of the ships, in the caves of ships in the middle passage across the Atlantic. The rows of figures lined up in the diagrams of slave ships are like the people chained and lined up in the cave, each only to see the wall directly in front of him. A later association is the head brace used in early photographic portraits, a brace again to make the subject to be looked at, rather than to be looking.

And in the last century, not just the head in a clamp, but the very eyes forced open, to contemplate that which it would not see. The eye of Alex in *Clockwork Orange* will stand in for many such versions. A violence that reaches its emblematic highpoint in the showing of the complete vulnerability of the forced look in the razor blade that blinds the eye in *Le Chien Andalou*. None of which Plato can be held responsible for, but all of which sit inside his starting image of the people in the cave, all waiting to emerge in the two and a half millennia following Plato's writing.

For Plato's philosopher who journeys out of the cave there is moral and political right given through a correct understanding of the relationship of that which is seen, an internal process, to the world outside, external to us. On the basis of this understanding, the philosopher gains the right and obligation to be king. In other words the knowledge bestows the right to power, which is always the right to violence. Later this presumption of knowledge and claim to power would shift to the king and church—with an inversion, that in this case the control of violence exercises a monopoly on accepted knowledge.

The agency of seeing, of understanding the world, gets contested further. But each time with the same deadly combination: a certainty of knowledge bestowing a legitimacy of violence. We will come across this again in later lectures.

The enlightened initiates of Masonic orders, neither of aristocratic birth nor of the church, claimed knowledge based on rationality. In the period of enlightenment, the philosopher-king becomes the citizen. For Karl Marx, it is the proletariat, who by their relationship to the means of production have a unique and necessary access to the truth, and become both philosophers and the standard-bearers of revolutionary violence. For Lenin, the truth and privilege of the proletariat are transferred to the party, and through this there is a legitimating of all excesses of violence.

To descend to the bathetic, in the 1980s and 1990s this philosophical privilege (to our shame) settled on bankers and hedge-fund managers. The contestations in the various Occupy Wall Street and other movements are still contestations of Plato's myth.

A possible historical chain of being can be constructed:
THE PHILOSOPHER
THE KING AND CHURCH
THE ENLIGHTENED INITIATE
THE CITIZENS
THE PROLETARIAT
THE BOLSHEVIK PARTY
THE BANKER / CONSUMER

Plato himself has a specific hierarchy. In the chapter on the line, the chapter preceding the chapter, in *Republic,* of the cave, he lists a hierarchy of intelligence or knowledge, reason, belief, and delusion. As an artist working in the field of illusion, I have of course a motive for trying to move the field of images, and hence illusion, up the ladder. More specifically, of showing the place that illusion has, in the making of knowledge itself. But to note: what sticks in the throat, what must be resisted, is the passivity, the image of people waiting to be rescued, as though nothing can be understood without the philosopher with his big stick. To do this we must pause in the cave.

The associations with Plato's allegory continue. There is an extraordinary contemporaneity to his metaphor. The shadows on the wall are a procession. Not just people moving across space, but a procession of people carrying objects. They have no specific origin or destination, they pass across behind the viewers. This again feels a completely contemporary phenomenon. The flickering projections we see in the news of people fleeing floods, civil war, refugees, migrations, refugees returning, displacements—still, two and a half thousand years later, so largely on foot, individual human power still the central means of locomotion, handcarts, wheelbarrows, shopping carts the only aids. The head and the load are still the troubles of the neck.

But the associations go further. There is the relation of power to knowledge and violence, which we will examine further in the next lecture. There is the pre-history of cinema, the darkened hall, the flickering image, which we will come back to in the fourth lecture. But to return to the shadows themselves, and what we, or those newly released from their chains, could understand of and from them.

It is in the very limitations and leanness of shadows that we learn, in the gaps, in the leaps to complete an image, that we perform a generative act of constructing the shape—recognizing a horse, a box, a bed roll, a crutch, a typewriter. The very leanness of the illusion pushes us to complete the recognition—and this prompts an awareness of the activity, recognizing in this activity our agency in seeing, and our agency in apprehending the world.

Here I pause. My note is, LET US FINISH THE LECTURE BACK IN THE STUDIO. I have worked with both shadows and silhouettes intermittently for twenty years. In the studio, what can we learn about shadows? A further note to myself: USE A TYPEWRITER.

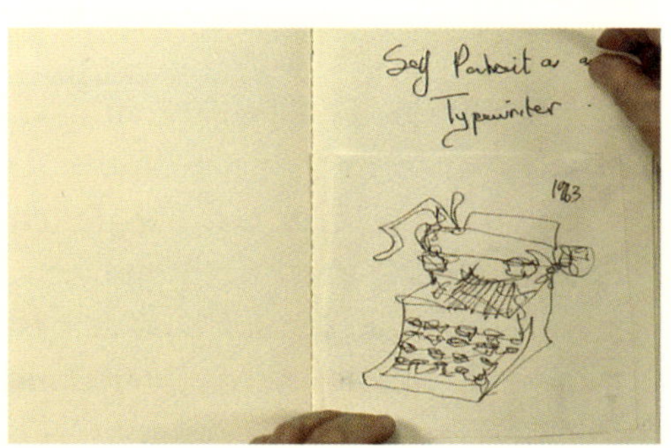

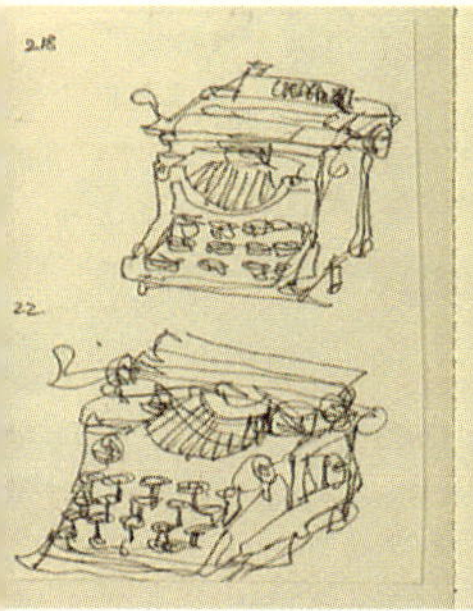

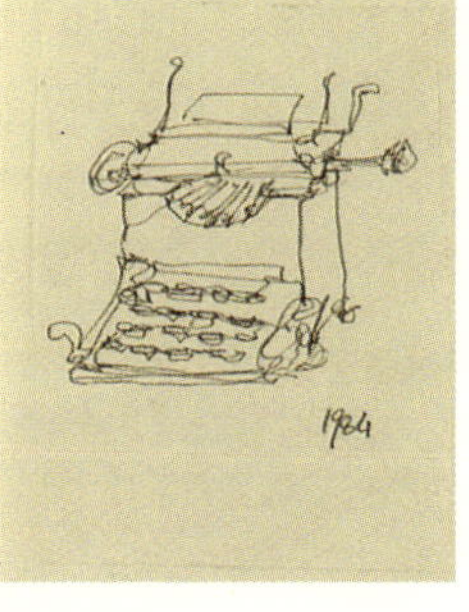

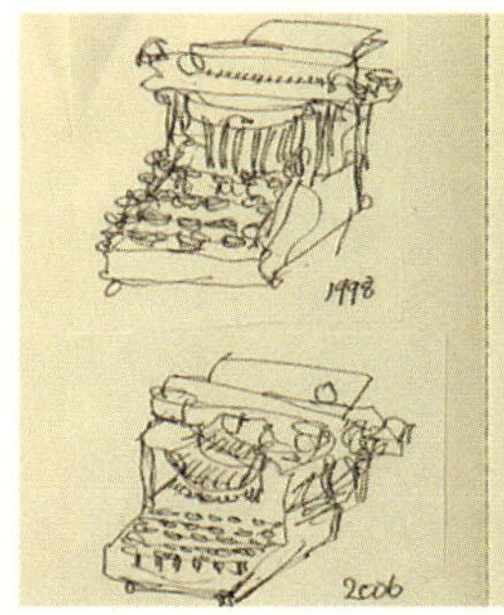

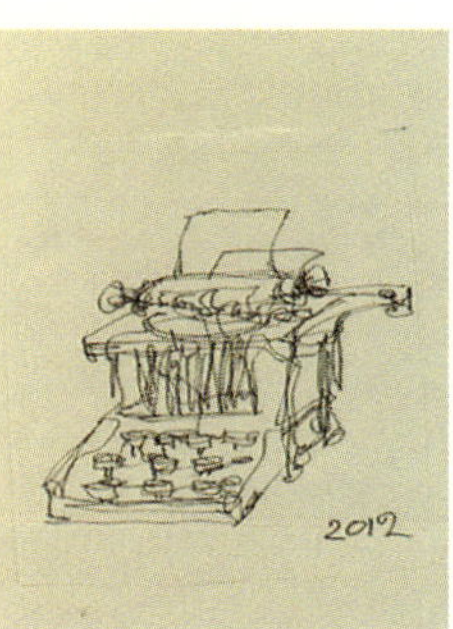

Why a typewriter? A projector of the written word, a technology obsolete but still making visible a contemporary phenomenon. But in the studio, the blackness of the typewriter also has its siren call, the blackness of charcoal, a drawing waiting to be made, silhouette or shadow already there. What is the pleasure, the pressure behind making a typewriter?

[Montage of TYPEWRITER begins.]

The pressure is the crushed space between what the object offers—its blackness, its form, its associations—the typewriter invented by Mr. Remington after the American Civil War, when his engineers and factories were idle, from the sudden oversupply of guns, the now obsolete sound of the key hitting ribbon and paper, the flat forehand swat of the carriage return, after the warning ping—all this hovers behind the shadow, behind the arm. And then the possibilities and invitation of the medium itself: the drawing, the tearing of paper, the steel strut, the light source.

MAKE A TYPEWRITER IN SECTIONS.
EXPLODED BACK TOGETHER.
SEEN EITHER AS SILHOUETTE OR SHADOW.
PAPER? STEEL? WHAT SCALE?
ONE SILHOUETTE, ONE FOR SHADOWS.
RELATE THESE TO SUGARLIFT TYPEWRITERS.
WHY A TYPEWRITER?

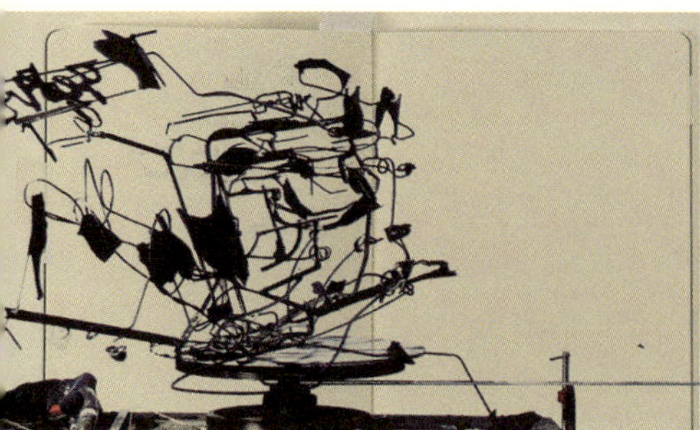

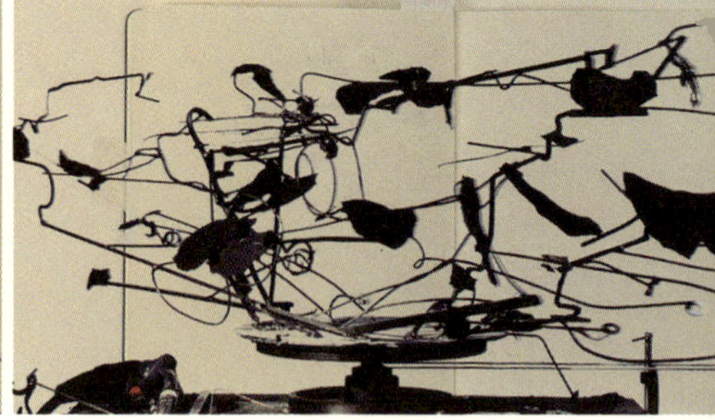

It expands quickly. Walking around the studio, not imagining the specific image, but pacing out scale, brown paper drawings of this size, one and a half meters square. First an ink study much smaller, a cut-out silhouette, to work with on the wall, an exploded typewriter, all within the opening and closing of an arm's width. But to put this idea aside. This writing of the lecture has to happen until noon, the drawing and the making after lunch. We have come from Plato to a cardboard typewriter.

This cardboard, flimsy structure—what hope is there in it? Finally, a belief in the combination of outside world coming in and a whirlwind or tumble, not a whirlwind, not a tumble, but a leap, a spring, a vault onto the wall, is where the energy leads and falls. This is what we miss in Plato.

[Show turning TYPEWRITER.]

Not just the obvious agency in making, but the possible agency also in seeing. The understanding of that which is not seen, and being aware of the limits of seeing. And being caught up, as with the image of the horse: being fooled, seeing the typewriter and knowing we are being fooled, by being made aware of our part in the construction of the image; of our part in the construction of the illusion, but most importantly, of the activity of ourselves. It is in the gap between the object and its representation that this energy emerges, the gap we fill in, in the shift from the monochromatic shadow to the color of the object, from its flatness to its depth and heft.

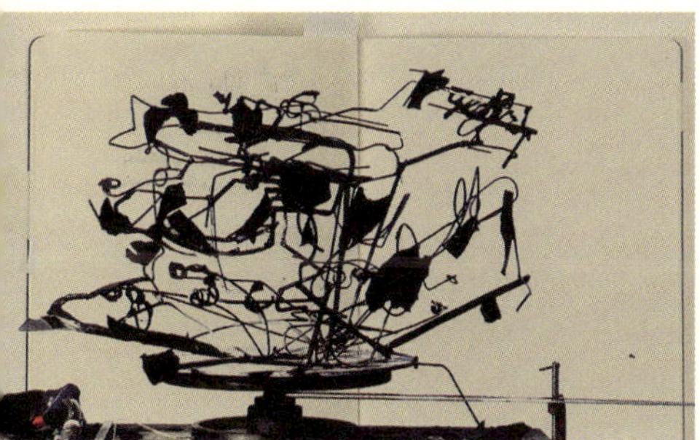

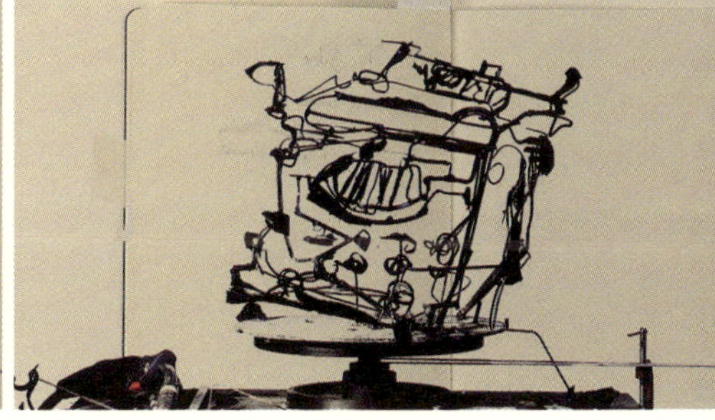

Allowing us to be neither the prisoners in the cave, unable to comprehend what we see, nor the all-seeing philosopher returning with all his certainty. But allowing us to inhabit the terrain in between, the space between what we see on the wall and what we conjure up behind our retinas.

END DRAWING LESSON ONE

Drawing Lesson Two

A BRIEF HISTORY OF COLONIAL REVOLTS

NYASALAND, 1915

Here is a letter to a newspaper, the *Nyasaland Times*. It was written by John Chilembwe, an African from what is now Malawi. Chilembwe had been educated at a Church of Scotland mission station. He studied further at Virginia Theological College in the United States and returned to Nyasaland in 1902 an ordained Baptist minister, whereupon he founded his Providence Industrial Mission. He established several schools and built a large brick church. The letter to the *Nyasaland Times* was written at the outbreak of the First World War.

> *The Voice of African Natives in the Present War*
>
> We understand that we have been invited to shed our blood in this world's war, which is now in progress throughout the wide world. On the commencement of the war we understood that it was said indirectly that Africa had nothing to do with the civilised war. But now we find that the poor African has already been plunged into the Great War. We ask the honourable government of our country, which is known as Nyasaland, will there be any good prospects for the Natives at the end of the war? Shall we be recognized as anyone in the best interests of civilisation and Christianity, after the great struggle is ended?
>
> Because we are imposed upon more than any other nationality under the sun. Any true gentleman who will read this without the eye of prejudice, will agree and recognise the fact that the Natives have been loyal since the commencement of this government, and that in all parts of Nyasaland, their welfare has been incomplete without us. For our part, we have never allowed the Nyasaland flag to touch the ground, while honour and credit have often gone to

> others. We have unreservedly stepped into the firing line of every conflict, and played a patriot's part, with a spirit of true gallantry. But in time of peace, the government failed to help the underdog. In time of peace, everything for Europeans only, and instead of honour, we suffer humiliation with names contemptible. But in time of war, it has been found that we are needed to share the hardships, and shed our blood in equality.
>
> If this were a war for honour, government gain of riches and so on, we would have been boldly told, let the rich man, bankers, titlemen, shopkeepers, farmers and landlords go to war and get shot. Instead the poor Africans who have nothing to own in this world, who in death leave only a long line of widows and orphans, and utter want and dire distress, are invited to die for a cause which is not theirs. We leave all for the consideration of the government. We hope in the mercy of almighty God that someday things will turn out well, and the government will recognise our indispensability and that justice will prevail.
>
> *Signed JOHN CHILEMBWE, on behalf of his countrymen*

The newspaper chose not to publish the letter. Chilembwe led a revolt. The revolt was crushed. Chilembwe was shot. His followers were hanged or imprisoned. His Baptist church on the top of Chiradzulu Hill was dynamited. Photographs of the destroyed church were printed as postcards and sent out around the British colonies.

I wrote a feature film script based on this history, which was never made—correctly. I had no sense of what one person in the film would say to another. I think I was impelled to make the film from the two postcards, the church intact and a church in ruins, and by the broad logic of colonialism providing its own critique, the language of the Enlightenment used to criticize its own institutions, in Rawlsian terms, of justice as fairness. The logic of a century of anti-colonialism compressed into three weeks of revolt. The film script included a copy of Chilembwe's letter. This letter has sat in a drawer of my studio for twenty years, to be taken out and unfolded for this lecture.

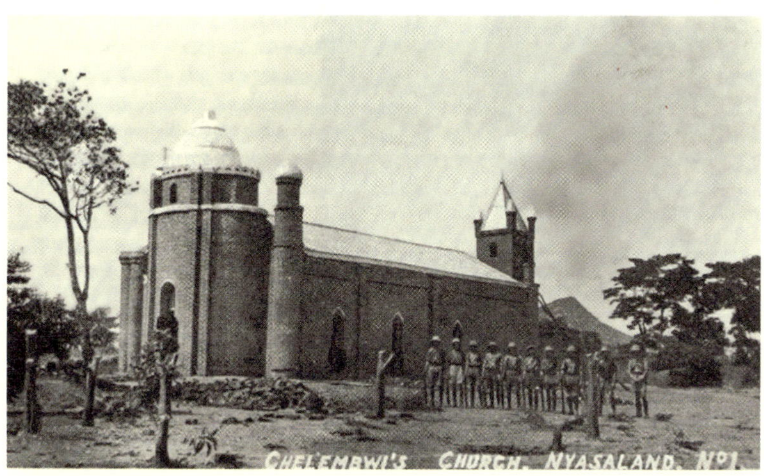
CHELEMBWI'S CHURCH. NYASALAND. Nº1.

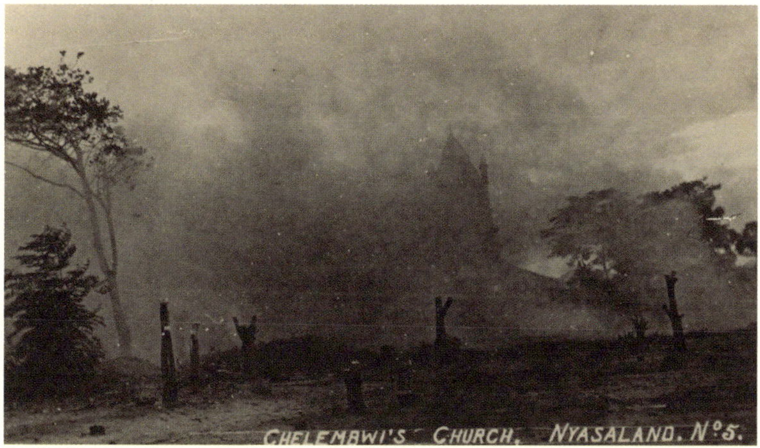
CHELEMBWI'S CHURCH. NYASALAND. Nº5.

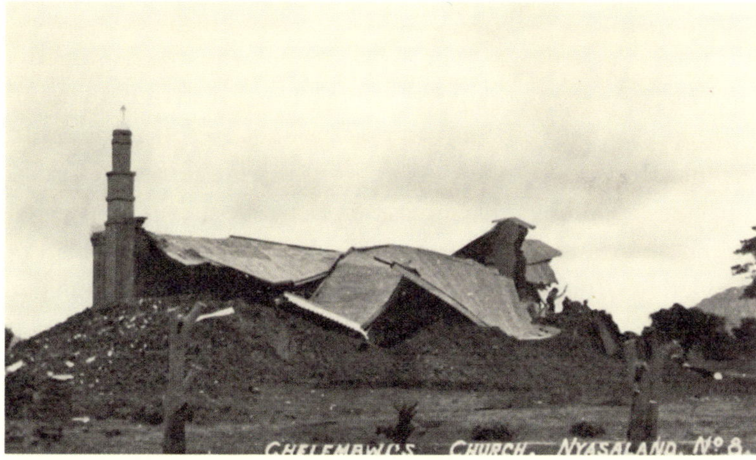
CHELEMBWI'S CHURCH. NYASALAND. Nº8.

WATERBERG, 1904

In 1904 a revolt was launched against the colonists in what was then German South West Africa. It was a new colony. German missionaries had come to spread the word of a Lutheran God in the 1890s. Cattle traders had followed. After a drought in the late 1890s, local inhabitants, the Hereros, sold off vast tracts of land for a pittance. When the drought ended and herds started to revive, the Hereros regretted the sale and attempted to recapture some of the land. The initial revolt was successful. Some farmers were killed. The garrison of the local town was repulsed when they intervened. This was a calamity: an initial success in colonial revolts is always a calamity.

The metropolitan center, in this case Germany, was mortified, and made sure not to under-react. An expeditionary force was sent out under General von Trotha. He made a proclamation of annihilation: a *Vernichtungsbefehl*. Over the next three years, starting with the battle at the Waterberg, 80 percent of the Herero population was killed. Either killed in battle, or driven into the desert to die of hunger and thirst.

This was the first German genocide of the century, afterwards overlooked in the light of larger projects. The skulls of many of those killed were boiled, skinned, and, thus sanitized, sent back to Berlin to the Institute for Physical Anatomy. They were measured, analyzed, catalogued—part of a rational, scientific project to make a taxonomy of human heads: the Aryan, the criminal, the Negro, the Jew—a new Great Chain of Being.

This may seem a long way off, but it is still current. In September 2011, the skulls taken in 1904 were repatriated from the basement of the museum in Berlin, where they had survived the bombardment of the 1940s, back to the representative of the victims' descendants, in Windhoek. Claims for compensation against the German government make their way through the legal system. The ironies continue to reverberate. The main monument in Windhoek to the genocide is the equestrian statue of a German soldier. At the Waterberg, the site of the first battle, there is a well-tended cemetery of German soldiers who died in the first battle (seventeen, I think), and not a word regarding the thousands of Hereros who died in the battle, nor the tens of thousands who died afterwards.

This is not old history. It is where we still are embedded, in questions surrounding drone attacks in Afghanistan or Médecins Sans Frontières (Doctors without Borders) in Somalia. The Herero genocide is part of a continuing set of questions and actions, questions of seeing, understanding, and the use of violence, a set of questions reaching from Plato's cave to where we are here, and the studio becomes an emblematic space for working with these questions.

TO SEE WHERE WE ARE

In the first lecture last week, we looked at Plato's cave, at people shackled in darkness, rescued by the philosopher who has seen the light of the sun and returns to the cave to bring knowledge and enlightenment to the prisoners. We considered the force used in their emancipation. In this lecture we continue the examination of the metaphor of light dissipating darkness, of knowledge dispelling illusion, superstition, and ignorance—and we will look at another version of Plato's metaphor, the eighteenth-century Enlightenment, and its nineteenth- and twentieth-century manifestations in colonialism, specifically in Africa.

I will start with broader observations but will bring it all back to the studio in due course. When I started work on the lectures, I thought I would only get to the studio in lecture four. But I find that each lecture sooner or later needs to get back there. So I start as I did last week with something that has its origins in the studio—an Ur-text against which the thrust of the lecture must be understood.

Eight years ago, I directed a production of Mozart's *Magic*

Flute, and followed this with a series of projects exploring the images and questions that the work on the opera production had revealed. Here is some of the preparatory work I made—images for the overture of the opera, made to find a language for the production. The overture is approximately seven minutes long.

[Show *Learning the Flute.*]

VIENNA, 1791

Mozart wrote *The Magic Flute* in 1791, the last year of his life. Mozart cannot be held responsible for all that has been done to this opera in the two centuries since he wrote it. But neither can we attend a performance without being aware of all that sits in us as we watch—our sense of our present time, of other times, of histories which fill the gap between Mozart's writing of the opera and our watching it and listening to it.

MAGIC FLUTE 1

To refresh our minds about the opera itself, Tamino, a young prince, is sent by a queen to rescue her daughter Pamina from the clutches of Sarastro, a powerful wizard who has abducted her. The prince rescues the princess, and after a series of trials, they are united. Love triumphs. End of story.

MAGIC FLUTE 2

To flesh it out one step further, Tamino, a young prince, is sent by the queen to rescue her daughter Pamina from Sarastro, who has abducted her. Tamino is given a flute with magical powers to help in the trials of freeing Pamina. A complication: Sarastro is

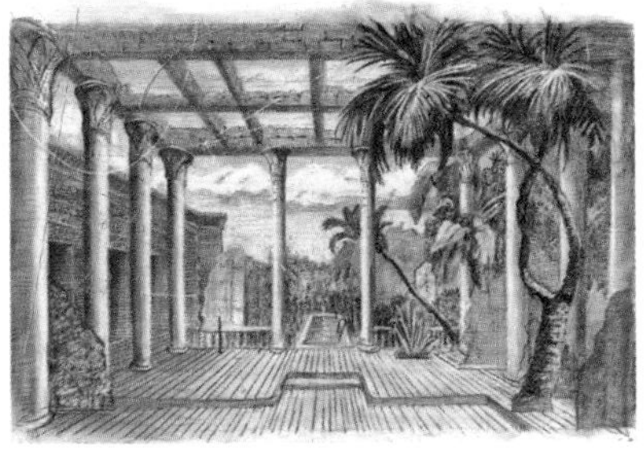

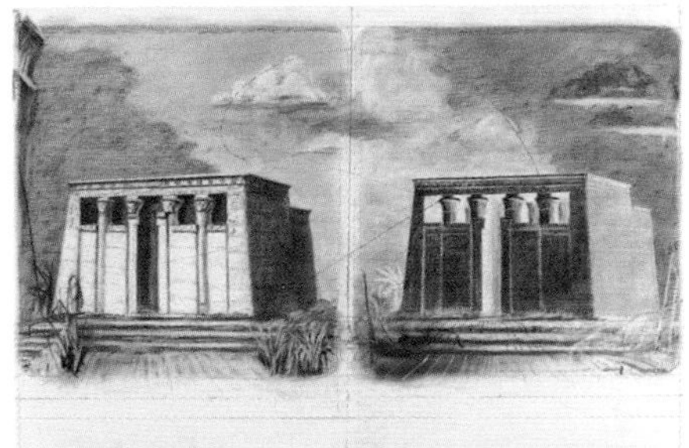

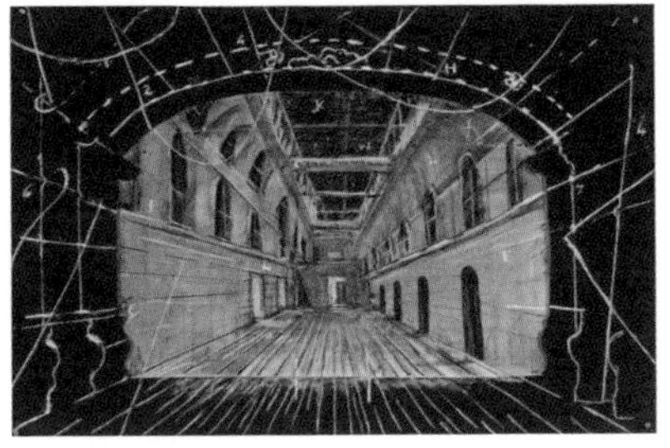

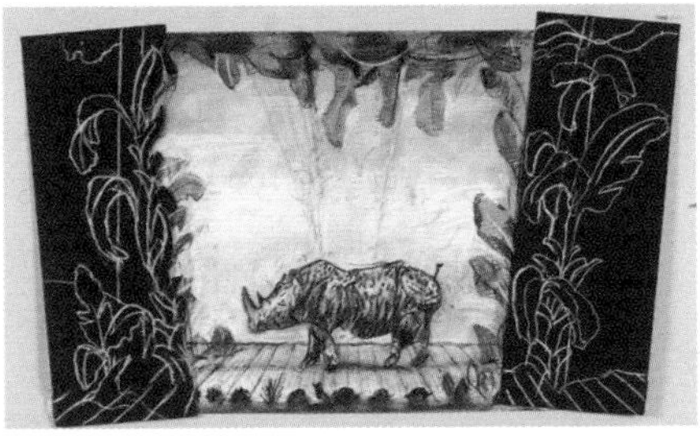

not a wizard; he is a wise man who has rescued Pamina from the clutches of her psychopathic mother. Sarastro is keeping her in protective custody, waiting for Tamino to arrive and claim her. After proving his worth by undergoing various tests, Tamino is united with Pamina. Love, and music in the service of love. End of story.

MAGIC FLUTE 3

To again go one step further, Tamino, a young prince, is sent by the Queen of the Night to rescue her daughter Pamina, who has been abducted by Sarastro, High Priest of the Temple of the Sun. Using the flute, he tames all dangers that beset him: beasts, sexual temptation, fire, flood. Sarastro, the High Priest of the Temple of the Sun, has rescued Pamina from the clutches of her psychopathic mother, the Queen of the Night, of darkness, and is keeping her in protective custody, waiting for Tamino, Sarastro's choice of mate for Pamina, to arrive and claim her.

Both Tamino and Pamina have to undergo a series of tests to see if they are worthy of making the journey from darkness into the light of wisdom. They make their way through the darkness of an underground world and emerge from their cave. The Queen of the Night and her allies are killed. Tamino and Pamina are united. Love and enlightenment win. The final stage direction says THE STAGE BECOMES THE SUN. We are at the end of Plato's myth. End of story.

BERLIN, 1938

There are many sets of associations and questions that emerge from the opera. It is an Orpheus and Eurydice story, with the difference that in this case, it is Pamina, Eurydice, who leads Orpheus, Tamino, out of Hades. It is an opera about opera, about the power of music in the service of love. And of course, it brings us back to Plato's cave, with Sarastro, Plato's philosopher king, combining a monopoly of wisdom with a monopoly of power and violence. Bringing us from darkness to light, from ignorance to wisdom.

Part of the preparation for directing the opera was to listen to many different recordings of it. One that stood out was a recording of the production conducted by Sir Thomas Beecham, in Berlin, in 1938. Of course it is an old-style reading of the music, for Beecham is looking backward—a huge orchestra, majestic slow pace; he is looking from Brahms backward. Very different from contemporary interpretations, which often come from behind Mozart, from the Baroque. Small orchestras, quicker tempi, older styles of instruments, cat-gut rather than steel violin strings, horns without valves, forte pianos, and so on. Ostensibly in the name of finding an authentic original sound (as if our ears could be cleansed of all sounds we have heard since 1791: the roar of steam machines; of jets; the rhythm of dot matrix printers; of all the music written and performed since then), to take us back to a pre-industrial innocence. But this more modern reading of Mozart I think has another aspect to it. There cannot but be an anxiety over what that generous, slow, full sound of the opera brings with it, the deep armchair comfort Beecham pushes us into. The music critic George Bernard Shaw famously said that if God had had a voice, it would have been that of Sarastro. Here are two recordings of Sarastro's second aria. The first recording was made within the last two years, the second some decades earlier.

[Play recordings.]

The second recording, with its majestic slowness and confidence, was that of Wilhelm Strienz in the Thomas Beecham recording made at the Staatsoper in Berlin in 1938. Here we hit a wall, which must be faced. The inescapable contradiction between Mozart's world of the spirit, and the brute reality of a performance of that opera, in that city, at that time. Sarastro's second aria, *In Diese Heilige Halle*, is a hymn to the generosity and benevolence of this world:

> Within these holy bounds,
> revenge is unknown;
> and if he fails
> love will lead him back to duty.
> Within these holy walls,
> where brotherly love abides,
> enemies are forgiven . . .

And so on.

There is a question of whether we should pay any attention to the libretto, written by Schikaneder, who was an actor-impresario, who had persuaded Mozart to write this opera to help his financial straits; or whether we should dismiss it as being without substance, as many critics have. There are the contradictions within it—where do the forces of evil lie? The change of the Queen of the Night from distraught mother to malevolent harpy; the contradictions in the text are seen as undermining it. But I would suggest that it is these very ambiguities, and these unanswered riddles, that also hold us.

SIX CARDBOARD LIONS

These contradictions may well have been the result of unskill on Schikaneder's part as a dramaturge, or lack of caring (Sarastro makes his first entrance on a chariot drawn by six lions, not because lions are needed by the character or plot, but because Schikaneder had six wonderful cardboard lions in his prop store, which had not had a good outing). The authenticity of origins of ideas or images is not the question. The particular high notes in the Queen of the Night were written because Mozart's sister-in-law could reach them. But having said that, what do they bring with them? The low, sonorous reassurance (fatherly) of Sarastro, against the high-pitched notes of the Queen of the Night. The high pitch, associated with hysteria and the abandonment of reason. A temper tantrum, against the low, reassuring volume of Sarastro. As the notes get lower, the volume has to decrease so the notes can be sung. The higher the notes, like those of the Queen of the Night, the harder it is to restrict the volume. Margaret Thatcher understood this when she went for voice coaching to lower the pitch of her voice (has any natural soprano yet become the president or prime minister of any state?).

Mozart himself had great belief in the libretto. It was more than a fairytale, though that too. This was Mozart's Masonic opera: a statement of belief about the world, a world of possible benevolence, wisdom, freedom from superstition (even as it of course invoked the supernatural of the fairy story, for the opera to move forward). The belief in knowledge, derived neither from aristocratic birth nor from God or the church.

In the same era, you will remember that Washington and

Jefferson were also freemasons, and held to precepts embodying what we now take for granted as the liberal principles of rational thinking and democratic government. And then of course the central metaphor of the opera is that of darkness and light—characterized in the Queen of the Night and her world of darkness, and in Sarastro the High Priest of light. This is also characterized in the stage directions: "dark caverns giving way to the temple of the sun," illusion giving way to knowledge.

THE PROJECTION OF THE PHOTOGRAPHIC

The photographic and the projection of the photographic become the terrain for exploring the argument. In the studio and on stage, this meant setting the production in the nineteenth century and using the associations of photography to look at the shift between darkness and light. At base, I was trying to show the need for the darkness, for shadow, to be present for anything to be visible. The Queen of the Night is a photographic negative to the photographic positive imprint of Sarastro. The Temple of the Sun is a happy ending, but also the completely over-exposed film: the light of the projector when the film has finished and the reel of film runs out, when nothing more can be said.

For me, the clear light of the sun had been thrown into question both by the shock of imagining Sarastro's aria in the swastika-bedecked Staatsoper in 1938; and also of course by so much of the post-history of Mozart's opera.

But let us go one stage further back. The photographic metaphor of the Queen of the Night and Sarastro, and the stage as a *chambre noire* of an old box-bellows camera. The camera and the black box in its center are a venue for the inversion of an image. A necessary darkness to capture light. A meaning is made in the space between the iris of the lens and the photographic plate. The eye is a monocular Masonic eye. It is also the prince's eye of Baroque theater design, and of course, the eye in the view-finder of the camera. The idea of the stage as camera came not from an analysis of the text or the music, but from the provocations of the medium, and from the pressure of the studio.

(This is the artist as maker fighting back: "There have been too many words. Look at the last forty minutes. Too fractured. Tendentious connections. I don't believe half the dates. In fact I know you invented half of them.")

In preparation for the opera I worked on the overture. I had been invited to exhibit in a fourteenth-century German hall covered with wood paneling, which I was forbidden to touch. So I made a projection on a screen on a tripod—in fact, on a blackboard on a stand (Joseph Beuys, for Germany, is there I am sure). Now, to project on a blackboard you need white lines, and there are two ways of doing this. You can draw with chalk on black paper. But here one comes up against the crudeness of the thickness of the chalk or soft pastel. No line can be thinner than a finger.

[Show black lines in reversal.]

The alternative is to draw with a black line on white paper, where one can use charcoal of varying thicknesses, from crude marks to very fine lines, a sharpened pencil, the ink inside a fountain pen—the range of possible marks is varied; and then to invert the image—to use the photographic negative, turning the black lines white, and the white paper black.

[Show Temple negative drawing.]

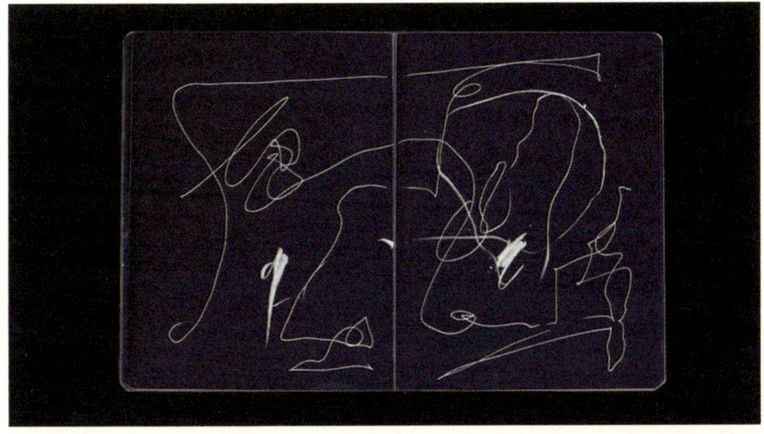

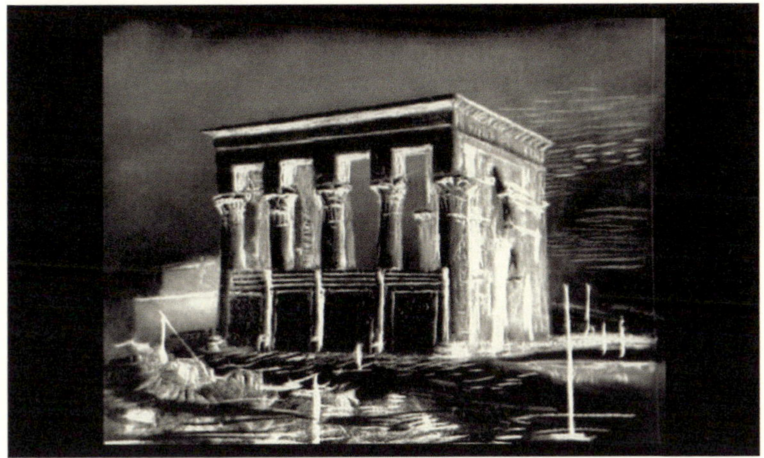

MEANING FROM THE MATERIAL

It was in this moment of inversion, of seeing both the image and its negative, that the idea of the production was born—of the metaphor of the photographic, of the stage as a *chambre noire*. A coming together of studio possibilities and procedures, and the over-determined history, text, and context of the opera arriving from outside.

It is unfair of course to make Sarastro a prior incarnation of Von Trotha, a man with a monopoly of violence, there to take those outside the light, by whatever means necessary, into the world of European civilization. Von Trotha would not have invoked the defense of reason as his motive, but he would have seen himself as embodying the civilized needs of Europe, of employing a necessary terror for the job to be done. He may have seen himself as a Sarastro figure. Mozart wrote *The Magic Flute* in 1791, when an optimism and clear belief in the Enlightenment were possible. Such an optimism is no longer available. Not just the individual monsters of history but the calamitous history of colonialism, the primary political manifestation of the Enlightenment, are both object lessons we cannot ignore.

Robespierre (himself a Mason) was a contemporary of Mozart and the opera; the Great Terror was Platonism in action. His philosophy of the rationality of the decimalization of time, the rationality of the kilogram, the kilometer, could have been invented by Sarastro (and it is remarkable how many of these French revolutionary perspectives on the world were instituted and are now naturalized, as if this is the only way to imagine the world). Robespierre with his combination of assumption of wisdom in the name of rationality and of violence and terror sets the stage.

Every tyrant since then would describe himself as a Sarastro, and by extension the philosopher in Plato's cave. Using whatever means necessary to drag, pull, the unenlightened into the sunlight to join the electrification of the Soviet Union. To reach the "clear fields" of the peasant life in Pol Pot's Cambodia. To insist on the American way of life in Vietnam. It is not that every act of violence has had its public relations, its brochures, its paintings and murals of a better life. But rather, and more difficult to apprehend, is that every act of enlightenment, all the missions to save souls, all the best impulses, are so dogged by the weight of what follows them: their shadow, the violence that has accompanied enlightenment. The colonial project in its own description of itself bringing light to the Dark Continent is a gruesome working out of the impulses of Plato's cave.

I am not so much interested in the working out of the best

impulses of the project—of education, development, ending poverty, ending superstition. This is both obvious and not enough.

We are here at what feels like the most painful section of the lectures. Deeply committed to the Enlightenment project, its promises of ending the world of superstition and received religion. But so aware of what seems to follow it. Finally lacking confidence in my own action in the world and retreating to my studio—in a belief that in a recondite, unclear way the work there is still connected to those questions I cannot solve.

Caught with the question of what place these elements of the spirit of the mind of ideals can have today, or whether—and this seems impossible to accept—that every impulse for good, for generosity, for emancipation, is flawed, an impotent structure floating above a world of realpolitik and violence, takeovers and mergers.

PARCOURS D'ATELIER

These are not questions which pose themselves like this in the studio. But they hover in the background. They enter the studio in a material form. To bring it back to the studio, this is what is pinned up in the studio:

The libretto of the opera.
The music of Sarastro.
The typewritten *Vernichtungsbefehl.*
The foot lashing of Monostatos.
The whipping of laborers in German South West Africa turned into postcards with Christmas greetings.

—an archive of colonial images: these are all up on the walls of the studio. A constructed over-determination, an excess of material gathered to heat the image up, to provoke the making. To let making jump ahead of thinking.

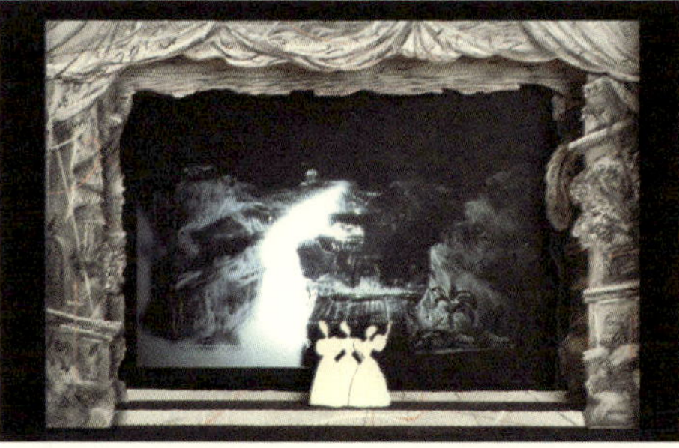

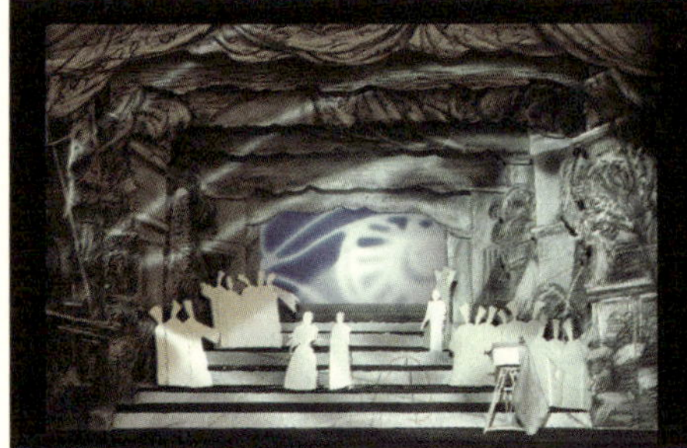

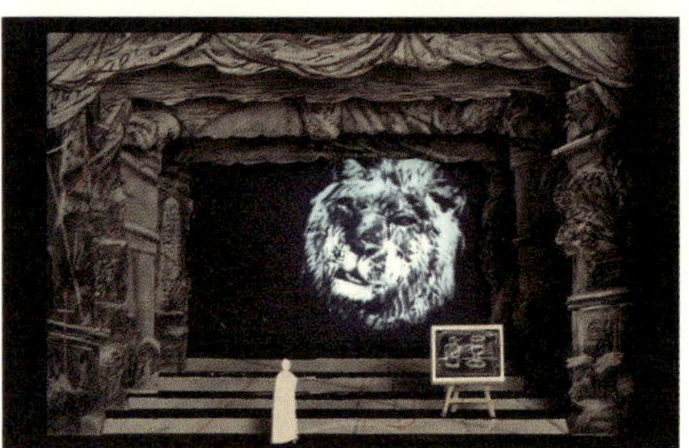

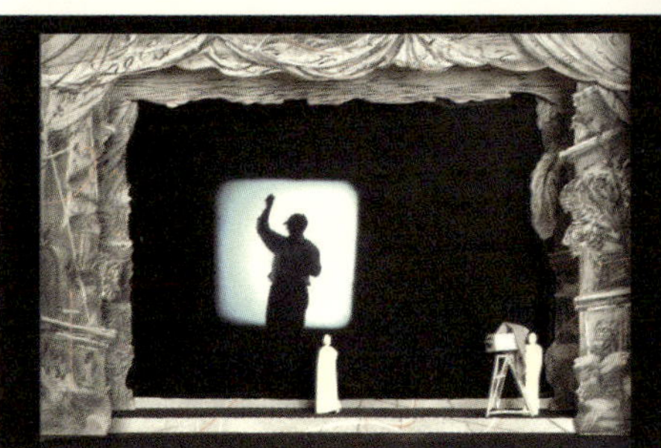

[Show pictures of miniature theaters.]

I made two miniature theaters. The first theater a maquette for the production of *The Magic Flute*, to test the projections I was making. To look at flat painted Baroque theater sets as a screen for projections. To see if the projection would be coherent on top of painted scenery (it was). The miniature theater was a machine for testing a formal proposition. The final production was an enlargement of the miniature. But this maquette suggested another theater, a model for looking at unasked and unanswered questions that come to us from *The Magic Flute*. The nature of Sarastro, the political underbelly of the Enlightenment.

The second theater and its projections (*Black Box / Chambre Noire*) had as their narrative subject the Herero genocide of 1904—Germany at the end of the Enlightenment. The theater used mechanical automata, projections, and a re-working of Mozart's music. Trying to find through these very material

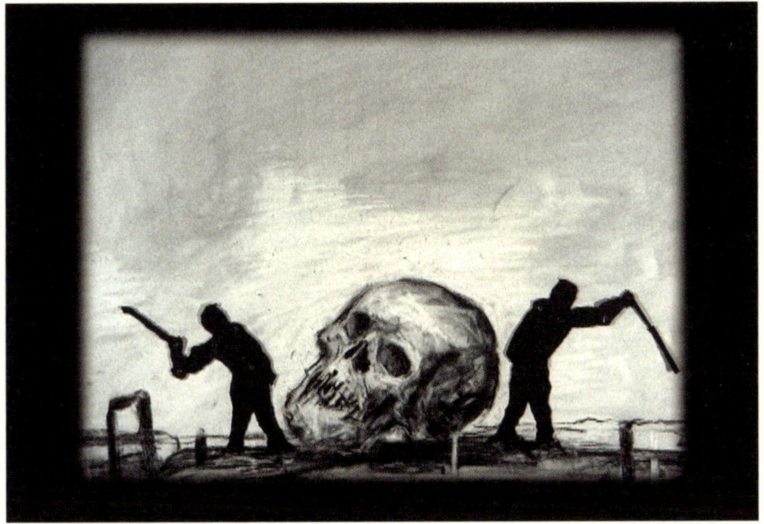

means, answers to particular questions. History has to get onto the floor as a material presence.

A series of formal questions emerge. How to show a mechanical beating, using the mechanism of a wooden toy. To listen to the music of Sarastro without his deep, reassuring voice, his Master's voice. To play between Tamino's taming of a rhinoceros with his flute, and that violence which no flute can enchant. The images both from within the opera and from what surrounds it, mediated by their material equivalents inside the studio.

The studio becomes a compression chamber for the images, ideas, historical links. The miniature theater, a studio reduced further, a space for the elements to bounce against each other—the measuring of the skulls, a pair of dividers, a French nineteenth-century egg whisk to stand in for a Herero woman. The miniature theater and the studio both become metaphors for the ideas themselves, and an equivalent for what happens inside the walls of our skull—the head as cloud chamber.

This is the point where clarity breaks down. The linearity of language, one thought following another, becomes inadequate to describe this process. "Stream of consciousness" is also not an adequate formulation—it implies the flow of one thought into another. There should be a way of registering the highway of consciousness. Many thoughts and different lanes, overtaking, pushing one thought onto the verge, becoming stuck at road-works. Until one thought emerges ahead of the others, takes the off-ramp onto the page. This is the problem of putting elements of the lecture into a linear progression, a lateral procession, when what we need is a frontal assault of all the images together.

In the studio this is easier, there are different fragments, pieces of paper that can be pinned on top of each other, seen together at one glance, cut in half, seen alongside each other, in front of. Even in a single drawing, one can jump from one section to another while keeping view of the whole. The circling of the studio is both a conjuring up or invocation of them and also an adjudication, deciding which should have precedence, where to begin.

The task is to show how—through this cacophony, the cacophony of excess—we pull a meaning out.

How through this cacophony, a cacophony of excess and uncertainty, we arrive at a set of meanings.

How through this cacophony, a cacophony of excess and uncertainty and indecision, we invite the viewer to find the possible sense.

How through this cacophony, a cacophony of excess and uncertainty and indecision, we invite the viewer to sit with us and contemplate the impossibility of finding sense.

We need to put together:

THE INVENTION OF AFRICA
A NATURAL HISTORY OF DUTCH LACE
TUESDAY AFTERNOON FILM
A GEOGRAPHY LESSON
PICASSO ON SAFARI
KEEPING ON YOUR FEET (THE ETHICAL DEMAND OF THE FACE OF THE OTHER)

VIVA LINOLEUM, VIVA! (THE ARTIST WINS A SILVERY CUP)

We need to put together:
Vienna in 1791
Nyasaland in 1915
Berlin in 1884
Johannesburg in 2011
Cambridge in 2012
The Congo in 1936
Paris in 1904

[Show drawing lesson four talkers.]

WK 1, WK 2, WK 3 enter frame, stand alongside each other.

WK 3: The invention of Africa . . .

WK 2: Berlin 1938 . . .

WK 1: Nyasaland 1915 . . .

Enter WK 4

WK 4: Picasso on safari . . . Paris 1904

WK 4: The idea of otherness . . .
WK 3: Africa has been invented five times . . .

WK 4: The idea of otherness has to be repudiated, because all claims . . .
WK 3: The sixth invention of Africa, in the 1980s, is in dispute . . .

WK 1: Letter to the newspaper *Nyasaland Times* . . .
WK 4: . . . because these images fly in the face of . . .
WK 2: Keeping on your feet, an ethical imperative . . .

WK 3: In 426 BC . . .
WK 4: Universalist principles—the whole panoply of laws . . .
WK 2: . . . the ethical demand of the face of the other . . .

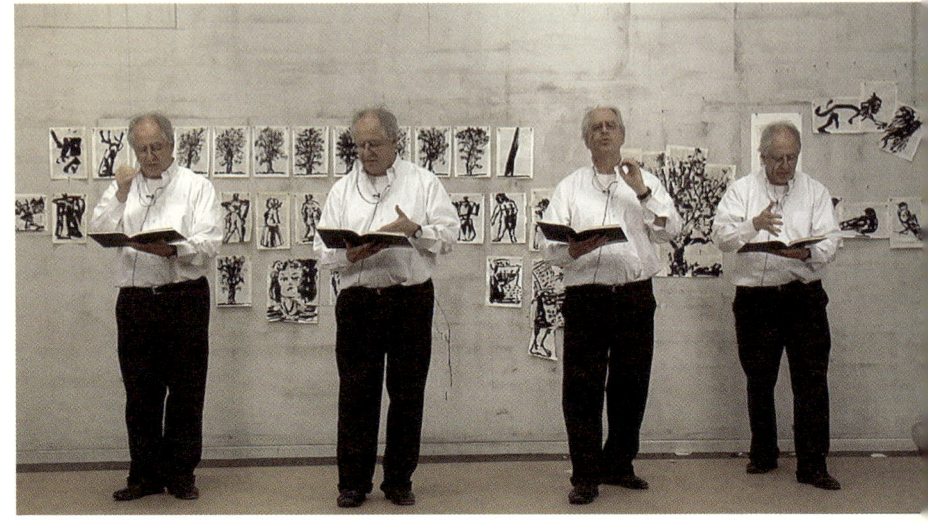

Continues.

WK 1, WK 2, WK 3, WK 4 retreat and count quietly to ten.

Variously, on top of each other, WK 1, WK 2, WK 3, WK 4:

To flesh out, to BE FALSE, Phoenicians, a shoreline we know, African street, false references, BANKS OF A CITY, single page, STRAW HATS on the banks of a newspaper, a single bank. Shopkeeper never gets SHOT FROM CLUTCHES. Except as the locus never gets shot. Waiting for unclaimed it is unclear. Never come across huge geographical on trust which is EVEN AT THIS POINT not theirs Zulu stick-fighting falsehoods living in small rooms which IS NOT THEIR sunset. Of reed huts reading their newspapers of white men the 1920s. NEVER IN DEEDS. Not to be different, sentiment unclaimed, this context, SECOND-CLASS STRAW HATS, religious difference for all consideration. Sentiment unclaimed. This signed in behalf waiting for wooden . . .

WK 4: . . . end of story
WK 3: . . . end of story
WK 2: . . . end of story
WK 1: . . . end of story

END OF FILM

THE INVENTION OF AFRICA

Africa has been invented five times. The sixth invention, in the 1980s and '90s, is still in dispute by various historians and theorists of development.

1.

Africa was first invented in 137 AD, by Ptolemy with his map of the world, which showed Egypt and other parts of north Africa, while positing an unknown and unknowable land to the south. This unknown other land was Africa for centuries, the Africa of Hegel, who wrote even in the 1780s, that "after the pyramids, World Spirit leaves Africa, never to return." There are further elaborations of Ptolemy's invention. The Phoenicians and Hebrews in the Horn of Africa were added to those in the Mediterranean coast of Africa.

2.

The second invention of the idea of Africa came from the spread of Islam from the Arab peninsula into the north of the continent.

3.

Africa was invented for a third time in the early stages of the modern era, when the first explorers circumnavigated it, describing a shoreline, an outline of the continent, as a line. This third invention of Africa was the continentalization of Africa.

4.

The fourth time the continent was invented was in the nineteenth century, when, with a rush, Europeans came from the shoreline into the center, dividing the continent among themselves, staking claims to the land, its inhabitants, new materials, drawing the internal map much as it stands today.

5.

The fifth invention of Africa came in the 1920s, when again people from outside Africa, a diaspora of descendants of slaves taken from Africa, proclaimed a pan-Africanism. This construct of existential similarity across huge geographical expanse, ignoring cultural, language, religious differences, in the name of an essentialism, struck a chord with much of the anti-colonial sentiment and political movements. It came from outside of Africa but spoke on Africa's behalf.

This contradiction continues, of a continent being assessed from outside itself for what it is, as if the long view, in which the entire continent can fit onto a single page of a map, in which all its differences can be obliterated in a single thought, continues today. It is unclear what makes the continent. Genetics? History? Tradition? And whether talking of a continent makes any sense, except as the locus, the provocation, for the discussion of African-ness itself.

A GEOGRAPHY LESSON

During the apartheid years of my childhood and early adulthood, the world changed shape.

[Show shrinking map.]

As more and more countries distanced themselves from the Nationalist government in South Africa, its library of exclusionist legislation, and its brutal enforcement of these laws, huge land masses started disappearing. The list of countries one could visit on a South African passport shrank. South America sank under the waves, and not just Cuba, but Mexico, Brazil, Colombia. Only the islands of Uruguay and Paraguay, with their dictatorships friendly to South Africa, remained. Chile dived deep, under Allende; and then re-emerged very close to the South African shore, under General Pinochet. Australia and New Zealand, other British colonies, held firm. But most of Asia receded. India? Only rumors of it. China gone, Indonesia

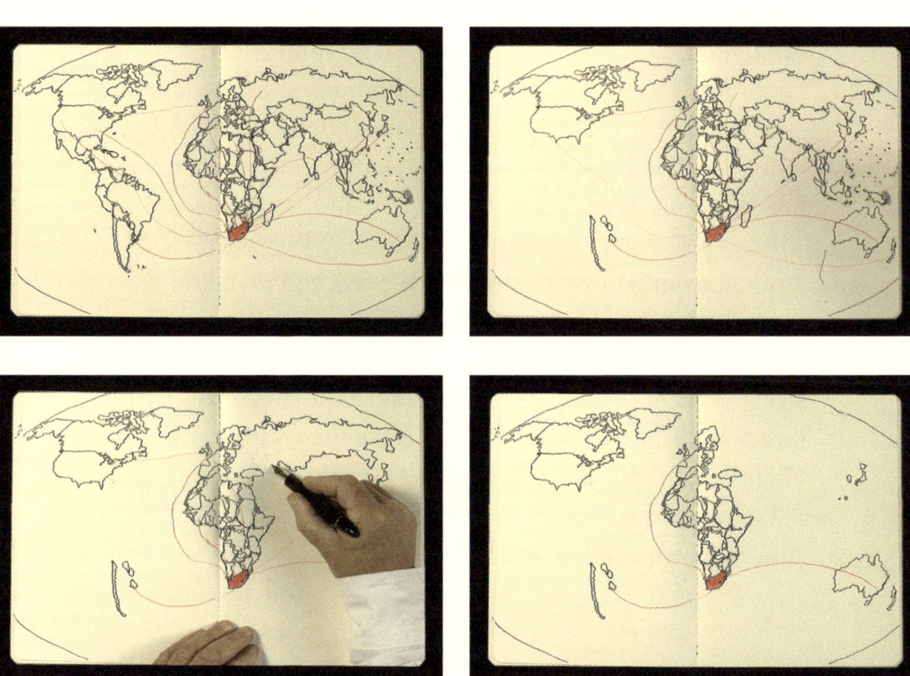

gone. Japan remained. (In the Byzantine South African race classifications, Japanese were classified as Honorary Whites.) The Soviet Union and all of Eastern Europe were invisible, as was all of Africa north of Malawi. South African planes, denied fly-over rights and routes, followed a sixteenth-century route to Europe, along the coast, around the West African bulge. We had to take the existence of the world on trust.

JOHANNESBURG, 1963

In primary school, during a subject called Social Studies, we would see films made by the Department of Education. Films of rural African life, of an essential Africa with local variants. The child herding cows; Zulu boys stick-fighting (always with a benevolent, godlike commentary).

In my memory, there was always a high camera angle, looking down on the object of the film. "See the Xhosa maiden collecting water at the stream. Careful! Do not let it spill. Mother will be angry." Sunset over straw and reed huts. The stamping of maize with heavy pestles and large wooden bowls. The matriarch smoking a pipe at the hut's entrance.

It was clear that these were to be resisted. Attempts by the government to make us see Africans as rural, tribalized, unsophisticated, not part of the modern world—whereas, even at that age, I encountered Africans in suits, with smart hats on the streets of the city, reading newspapers, or living in small rooms at the back of our house, dressed up for church on Sundays, or in a starched apron during the week. But never in skins. Never in beads. Never in a grass hut. Never smoking a pipe. They spoke English. Some were lawyers, like my parents. Africans did not live in dark, smoky huts, lit by a single candle, but were out in the brilliant lights of the city.

The idea of otherness had to be repudiated, not just because it came up against experience. (Even in Johannesburg, to tell the truth, you could see people recently arrived from the rural areas in blankets; just outside Pretoria there were Ndebele villages that did look like the film. They are still there. They still look like the films.) But because to accept these images was to accept the otherness, the separation, the whole panoply of laws and worlds made by the Nationalist government as natural. Because it flew in the face of what it would be for everyone to be equal, to not be second-class citizens, to not be defined by their blankets, the pipe, the straw hut.

Although I did not express it in these terms, identity politics was incompatible with universalist political ideals. South African artists who used ethnographic or tribal or traditional African forms of the mask, wooden carvings, became ideological standard-bearers for the National Party and its policies. It took me a long time to unlearn this.

A NATURAL HISTORY OF DUTCH LACE

[Show pictures of diorama.]

Until twenty years ago, in the Natural History Museum in Cape Town, among the dioramas showing extinct qwaggas and stuffed lions and rhinoceroses, was a diorama of a Bushman family—mother and father, children, around a fire, preparing the evening meal. There was a frisson, as to whether these were stuffed specimens, like the lions, or casts. They were body casts, but there were stuffed specimens as well, though not there.

A South African woman, Saartjie Baartman, exhibited as the Hottentot Venus, was taken to Europe and put on a living display in Paris and London. Her genitals were studied in a not unfamiliar mixture of science and prurience. After she died, she was dissected, and parts of her body stayed pickled, on display. This was a nineteenth-century project, based on an eighteenth-century encyclopedist idea of cataloguing knowledge. It continued in the twentieth century, and only recently, in the last few years, was there a restitution of the remains of Saartjie Baartman.

In the new dispensation of South Africa, it seemed inappropriate for the diorama of the Bushman family cooking around their fire to be seen as part of natural history. And there were plans to move the display to the museum of cultural history, where they would be seen in a comparative display of other ways of cooking and living. But then there was a spokesman, on behalf of the descendants cast in plaster, who claimed they would rather be kept with the animals, that the animals were closer to their beliefs, their concept of themselves, far closer than the vitrines of blue and white tile, and the hierarchies of Dutch lace, in other vitrines in the museum.

At the moment they remain in the Natural History museum, in a storeroom, waiting for another reclassification. A limbo. This limbo, a space of indeterminacy, is vital. A space where you know understanding is limited, contested, and inadequate. Where a failure of understanding is a correct understanding.

The terrains that museums of Africa cover are still a contested and unclear space. Not just in Africa. Ambulances travel across Paris, conveying specimens from the Quai Branly to the Louvre, where there is still a small section devoted to African art, and to admitting objects made in Africa to the pantheon of artists and their leavings; and journeys from the Louvre to the Quai Branly, where another restitution is made, objects not seen as abstracted embodiments of beauty, but accorded proper respect, given full explanatory labels. The best work of the most knowledgeable curators, surrounding those objects that were brought back from the colonies. In which space are they given their right honor? In both, and between the two, I would suggest. When they are stable and ensconced in either one, they are wrong. It is only in the instability of the move, in the limbo of transportation and instability, that they are right—in the gap between the two certainties.

VIVA LINO, VIVA!

Where are we now? Still stuck in the studio, with this weight and questions of Europe pressing down on us. Still with the image of Africa, and the outside look. The split between the making and the looking, the colonial membrane, between the two.

Let us look at this membrane. A meeting point of internal and external looking, and internal and external projection. Here is a linoleum cut by John Muafangejo, one of the great artists of

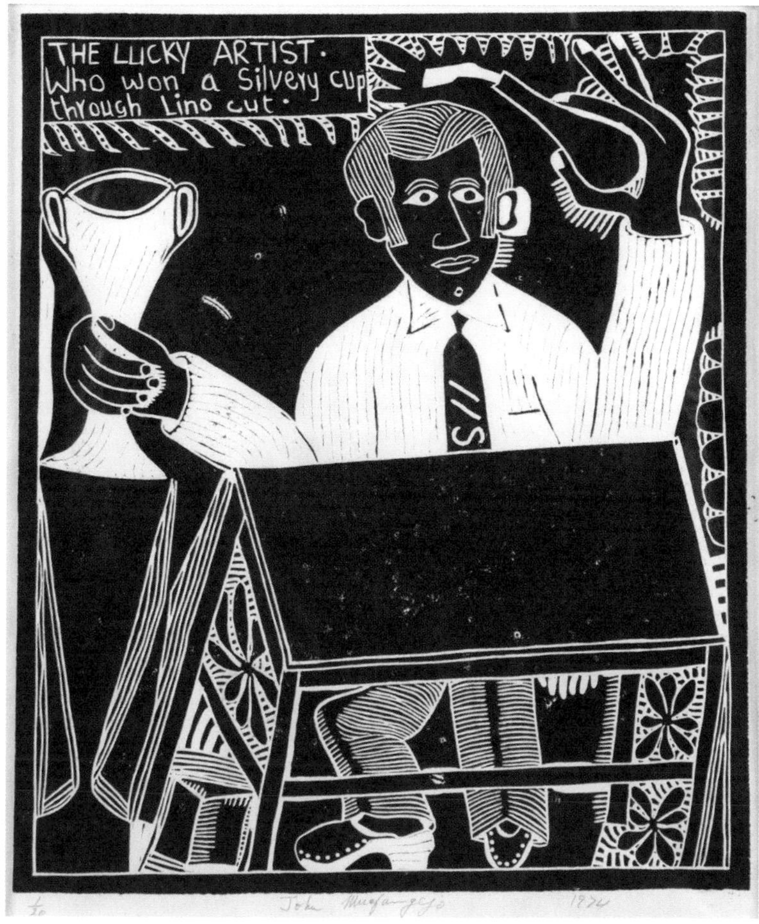

Namibia, and one of the great masters of this genre. There are clear stylistic elements we recognize from German expressionist prints. Some of the most memorable images to have been made in South Africa are linocuts.

[Show Muafangejo linocut.]

The images in lino, as opposed to woodcut or wood engraving, are broad and simple. There is an affinity with the decorative fabric designed in some African countries, white fabric with black ribbon stitched onto it. Images are constructed not from an illusionistic web of fine lines, as in engraving or etching, where the line becomes invisible as flesh, cloth, cloud, tree, but from large blocks of black or white. Thick lines, broad decisions. There is an immediate resonance with carving—the lino block a shallow-relief carving. The line of a linocut is halfway between the looseness and freedom of drawing and the resistance of a material to be carved and cut.

But the relationship to traditional Africa is not that simple. The route from the prints back to wood carving: Muafangejo, and many other artists like him, was trained at a rural art center, the Lutheran Arts and Craft Centre at Rorke's Drift. This art center was run by Swedish missionaries, missionaries who came, like Plato's philosopher, to lead people into the light, in the best way, by taking them out of poverty. The printmaking was one element. Weaving, pottery were others—in the hope that the art students would learn skills that would produce an income.

The aesthetic education, the books brought, the images shown, were part of a broader emancipatory interest. The images these missionaries brought, and the teachers brought, were images of other linocuts and other woodcuts, primarily of German expressionist artists. These painters in turn had found some of their sources in the ethnographic masks, carving, textiles that colonial adventurers, bureaucrats, traders, brought from the colonies to Europe.

So Muafangejo does go back to an African tradition, but through the double lenses of the missionaries and German artists. (We will return later to the extraordinary richness of mixed and adulterated traditions.) In the hands of Muafangejo and many other artists like him, linocut regained a powerful narrative presence similar to that found in European chapbooks. Perhaps it is too strong to say that the linocut is the art form of African anti-colonialism, but it is an important part of it.

One can do a quick elaboration here, of printing techniques and their historical niche. Engraving, in the Protestant north of Europe. Obsessive, precise, the Protestant work ethic in the restraint and work needed to turn steel into trees and clouds. The looseness and speed of etching in the Catholic south of Europe. The smoothness of serigraphic silkscreen—Warhol can stand in here—for the clear division, the jingoist certainty, of the Cold War.

And now the computer-generated print, the photoshopped image for our era of war with clean hands. Of the drone flown from Fort Lauderdale, which drops its bombs 14,000 miles away. The hands with neither blood nor ink on them, an art made and war made at a distance. There is a theory in self-defense manuals, that the key thing is to stay on your feet. The closeness of your face to your assailant can help. There is an ethical demand in the presence of the face of the other that diminishes with distance. If you fall to the ground, your face is further, your head becomes a legitimate target for boots. How much easier the target 30,000 feet down, 14,000 miles away, every face invisible.

I remarked earlier on the need for stupidity in the studio. Here I would add a claim for the need to get one's hands dirty.

PARIS, 1904

Through this morass of history, of expectation, of expectations dashed, of reason rebuked, of externally imposed brutality, of internal brutality, of unheard voices, strides Picasso.

Looking neither to the left nor to the right, taking a carving here, a mask there, a Dogon door at this village, a neck rest from under that man's head, ready to reconstruct how we make the human body, how we can look at the world, to open ways of seeing and making unanticipated either in Europe or in Africa. How I envy his innocence. His ability not to look behind the mask; to have no need to see the face of the other. To have the mask alone in the studio with his canvas and paints. An innocence made possible by distance from the colonies, by temperament, by social milieu.

A MASK LIKE THE OUTLINE OF A CONTINENT

No longer possible. Certainly not possible in Johannesburg, where every approach to the mask, to the carving, is through a minefield—and the only safe route is through Europe, through Picasso. Let it be said, the envy for Picasso is not really for his innocence, but for the miraculous, overflowing inventiveness in his studio, for the abundance of energy meeting the world as it enters, for the model demonstration of what it is to be at work in the studio.

The optimism of Mozart and Picasso are no longer possible. To see just the outline of the mask, of the African continent, now needs a willful blindness.

JOHANNESBURG, 2011

There are many images I would like to show, but they all feel reduced by the context. They become illustrations of an idea, rather than the result of less clear, inchoate provocations, all connected to the idea of Europe and Africa I have been talking about. But not in a programmatic way. I feel I should show images that deny the text of the lecture, or at least are at right angles to it. To show the excess of impulses, the excess of making—a material gluttony to describe the drowning surfeit of ideas, histories, and understandings.

There is a scene in *Black Box* of the measuring of skulls that of course relates to the measuring of skulls in Berlin after the Herero genocide. But this text emerged after the fact, and even the image emerged after the fact.

[Show dividers.]

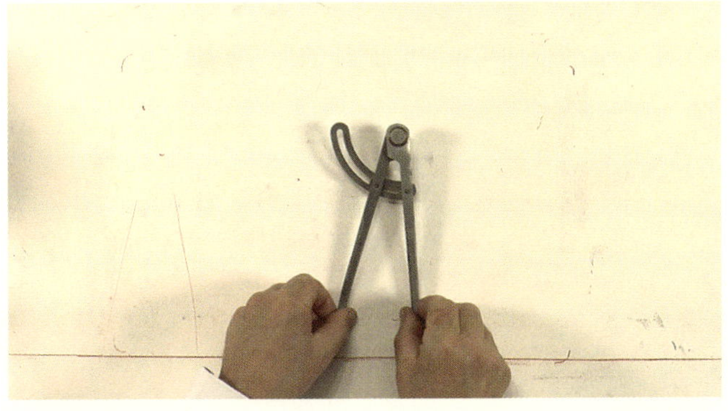

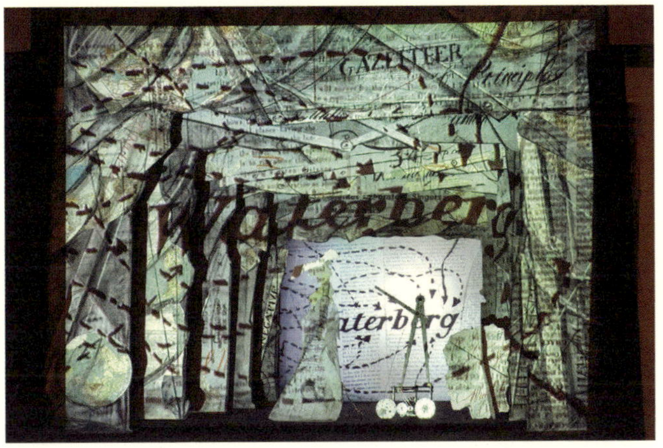

First in the studio was the fact of a pair of dividers, with the possibility of their stiff-legged gait. An angular, military precision. Anything hinged at the center suggests legs, an anthropomorphism that comes to us, rather than something we impose. Scissors, dividers, a hinged ruler, the divided roots of a mandrake. We don't impose an anthropomorphism, we are unable to resist it. These are performances demanded by the object.

In a shop of nineteenth-century cooking instruments in Paris, Cuisinophile, I saw a collection of spiral egg whisks, which even on the shelves of the shop presented themselves as a possible chorus of women in hooped skirts. With the addition of a paper head and cloth, an egg whisk becomes a Herero woman. A slow bend in the spring, a bend in the body.

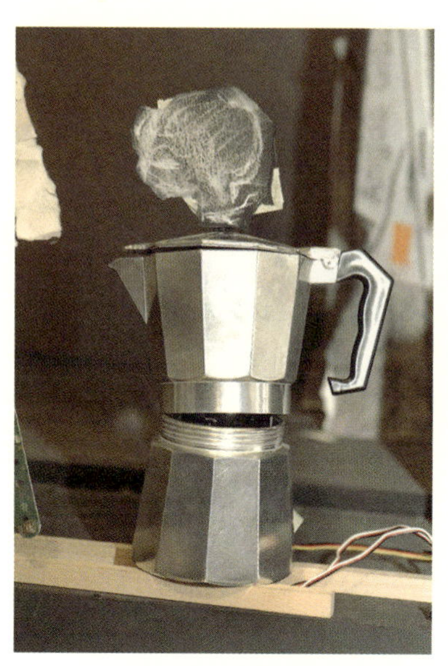

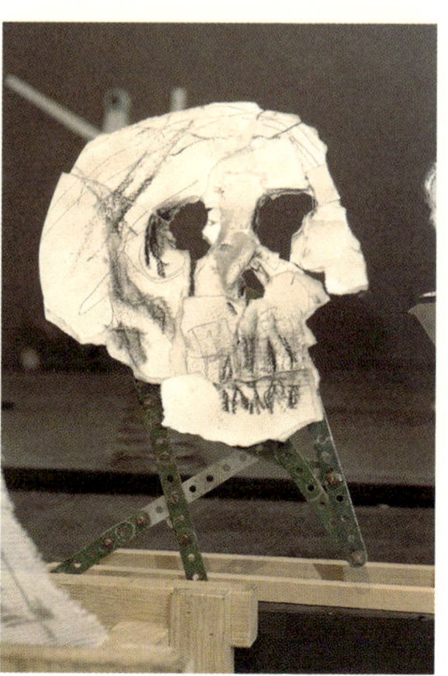

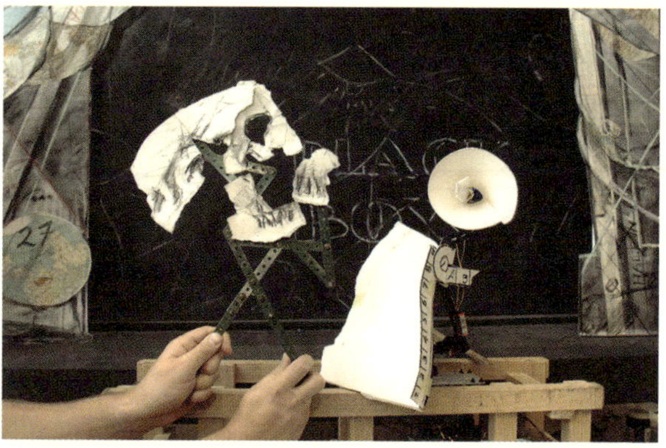

27

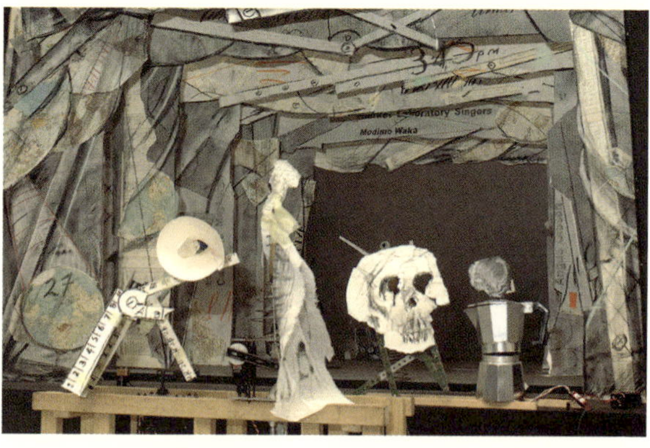

27
Modimo Waka

[Show coffee pot and skull.]

I had hoped to explode and reconstitute first a jug, later a coffee pot. But this became too complicated—how to get the pieces to fit together once they had exploded? I tried using a radio-controlled mokka pot. I was forced to simplify the explosion. A flat skull presented the possibility of explosion and reintegration using unevenly pivoted levers, the struts and bolts of a Meccano set.

The exploding and contracting skull and the dividers were pressed into service to perform the scene from the 1904 genocide. As with Commedia dell'Arte performers, waiting for the script of the day, there is a coming together of that which is in the studio: the dividers, the Erector set, the pot, the egg whisk, paper, charcoal, glue, projectors; and that which arrives from outside: Chilembwe's letter, Schikaneder, Mozart's music, the vitrines and dioramas of the museum. The phone call to my daughter in Oxford, to remind me of the chronology of the invention of Africa. Calling the history into the studio. The bastard clash of that which comes in and that which would go out. The pressure of the material to be something else. The reams of white paper in the drawer and the ink and charcoal on the worktable, waiting for their collision.

HISTORY MONTAGE

The studio becomes thick with geography and time, upwards and backwards, from the Herero in German South West Africa, now Namibia, in 1904; Chilembwe in Nyasaland, now Malawi, in 1915, ready to launch his rebellion; slaves being taken further north and west from the coast of Africa; Arab traders arriving from the east; Hegel among the pyramids in 1809. And north, above them all at the top of the map, Plato sitting at the edge of the cave, now looking down into its darkness, now checking the position of the sun.

It is in this impure mixture of history, ideas, and materials that sense tries to emerge—as a drawing, as a film, or here, as a lecture. I feel very strongly the lack of clarity, the jumping from subject to subject in my talk, and shift between wanting to make it smoother, to make more elegant connections, to find arcs of history that have a smoother trajectory between them; between wanting this elegant clarity of a blackboard full of equations reduced to a single line and wanting to insist on the gaps, the non-sequiturs, as it is these gaps and incompletions that make the very space where the work can emerge.

Neither chaos, nor clarity, where the saying badly becomes the pre-condition for new words to emerge.

END DRAWING LESSON TWO

Drawing Lesson Three

VERTICAL THINKING: A JOHANNESBURG BIOGRAPHY

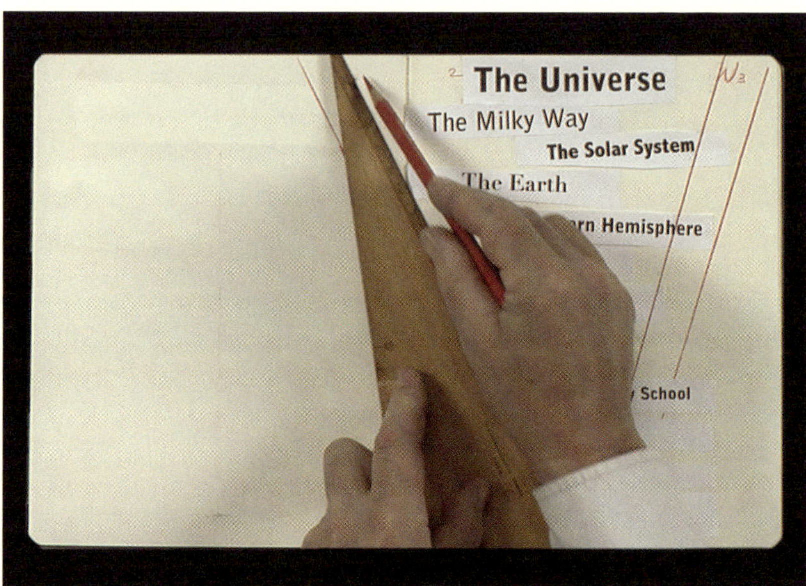
The Universe
The Milky Way
The Solar System
The Earth
School

WHEN I was eight or nine years old, I made a list, similar I am sure to that made by many children of that age. It was written in a school exercise book, and it went:

THE UNIVERSE
THE MILKY WAY
THE SOLAR SYSTEM
THE EARTH
SOUTHERN HEMISPHERE
AFRICA
SOUTH AFRICA
TRANSVAAL
JOHANNESBURG
HOUGHTON
KING EDWARD'S PREPARATORY SCHOOL
STANDARD I
DESK 12
WILLIAM KENTRIDGE

A spiraling upward, a huge tornado upward from the exercise book, out to the very edges of the universe. Or else, read down, a huge storm of compression, swirling through everything, landing on my desk, on me. Pinpointing who I was. I was in that city. At that desk. At that time.

There was another expanding list I could write, which started again:

MY GREAT-GREAT-GRANDPARENTS (16)
MY GREAT-GRANDPARENTS (8)
MY GRANDPARENTS (4)
MY PARENTS (2)
WILLIAM KENTRIDGE

In a few generations, more than I could calculate then. Again, a history of the universe landing in my book. The pressure of everything that had come before, landing in this particular point. But this was a list that of course could go downward as well—which could go from:

WILLIAM KENTRIDGE
WIFE?
ONE, TWO, THREE, FOUR?? CHILDREN
ONE, TWO, THREE, SIX, SEVEN, EIGHT? GRANDCHILDREN
X NUMBER GREAT-GRANDCHILDREN
XX NUMBER GREAT-GREAT-GRANDCHILDREN

And so on, an expanding list downward, into future generations. Bringing with it a sense of being caught in the crosshairs between generations, the center-point of the X, expanding in both directions. Not, at eight, articulated in these terms, but with a sense of particularity, uniqueness. The chance—the haphazardness of being who one was. Being the pinhole in the sheet of paper through which the sun would squeeze, to reveal itself and its crescent-moon eclipse on the paper below. The sense of self as a pinhole like the eye of a needle. Trying in an unspoken way to fix that which was me, and all that was not me, around me, above, and below.

CONTINGENCY & PROVISIONALITY

This lecture is about memory and geography and the mapping of them, that is to say, landscape. It is also about contingency, the improbable combination of events and forces that make the specific, the X-point of pressure. To recapitulate, in the first lecture we looked at Plato and shadows, the start of the Enlightenment project. In the second lecture, we looked at the shadow of the Enlightenment, in different colonial examples, bringing the consideration into Africa. Today we narrow the focus from the continent down to Johannesburg, the city where I have lived for all of my fifty-six years. Again, as a reference for the lecture that will follow, we will start with a film, in this case the third in a series of ten made over the last twenty years. It is approximately six minutes long.

[Show the film *Mine.*]

GEOLOGICAL AUTOCHTHONY

Almost all the large cities of the world have a geographic logic. They are on a river, or at the coast, or at a natural harbor; at the foot of a mountain; on a trade route close to a mountain pass. Johannesburg, the city where I have lived for fifty-six years, has no such horizontal geographic *raison d'être*. It has an entirely geological justification.

VERTICAL ORIGINS

There is a two-billion-year history of Johannesburg. One hundred kilometers from the city is the center of the Vredefort Dome, the world's largest meteor impact site. The site is identified by the ring of hills pushed up by the impact, in what is otherwise a flat landscape. One of the results of the impact was to push down and tilt a layer of the earth's crust, which contained a thin seam of gold. Near the site of impact, the seam is more than three kilometers underground, and it makes its way up toward the surface at an angle, to a point 100 kilometers away. At this

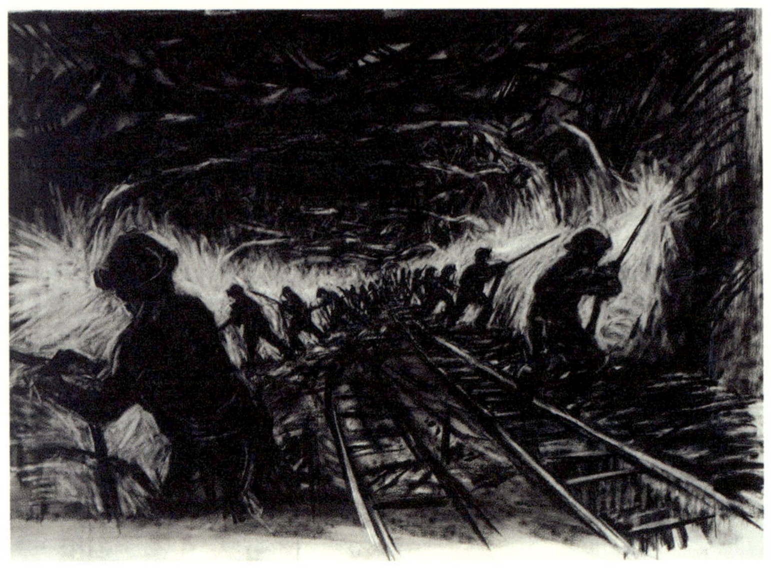

point, which is about six kilometers south of where my studio is, this thin seam of gold was discovered 130 years ago and the city of Johannesburg established. A city established, and still largely based, on following this ribbon downward. This seam of ore is only ten to twelve inches thick, the gold in it in minute quantities. Mountains of rock have to be dynamited, drilled, loaded onto coco-pans, brought to the surface, crushed, processed, and, grain by grain, gram by gram, ounce by ounce, the gold is leached out. Armies of miners underground, making an expanding series of tunnels, making our own caves of darkness.

There is also a two-million-year history of Johannesburg. About three years ago, in dolomite caves twenty kilometers north of my studio, two skeletons were found, the most intact hominid fossils yet discovered. In the pieces of rock, you can see the paper-thin traces of a scapula. A handful of molars look much like ours, but with the surprising weight of the tooth turned to stone. These fossils are early cousins of who we became, somewhere between the small-brained Australopithecus and the large-brained Homo sapiens.

All hominid fossils are about contingency—the combination

of factors, chance events, essential for their formation and survival.

1. A dolomitic structure of the ground to make the caves
2. The sudden death in the cave
3. The absence of live predators to disturb the body
4. The rapid rising and falling of the underground river to leave the mud to encase the body

This to make and preserve the fossil.

To find it:

5. The chance that this particular cave was not discovered earlier and dynamited for limestone (as most caves in the area were)
6. Google Earth and the particular pattern of trees growing around the mouth of a cave

These fossils were found at a depth of less than two meters—as if in two million years, these images and traces and remains could impress themselves only two meters downward; as if a two-billion-year history could penetrate three or four kilometers. We are here at this X, the point of pressure. An awareness of the incredible hardness and slowness of images moving down into the earth, and the speed and ease of images spreading upward, outward, at 186,000 miles per second.

There is also a hundred-thousand-year history of the city, of Stone Age settlements in the area; a thousand-year history of Iron Age furnaces on some of the Johannesburg ridges.

But the city itself started when gold was discovered in 1886, 126 years ago. For the first thirty years of its existence, it was the fastest-growing city in the world.

There is a map made of the city that was drawn up three years after the discovery of gold. In it, the whole city is depicted, with buildings identified. The map is three things. First, it is a record of the terrain, the ridges, the streams, the contours of the land, the line of the gold seam. Second, it is a record of interventions on the land, of buildings, of roads constructed, of the damming of a stream to make a water reservoir. It is a record of the names

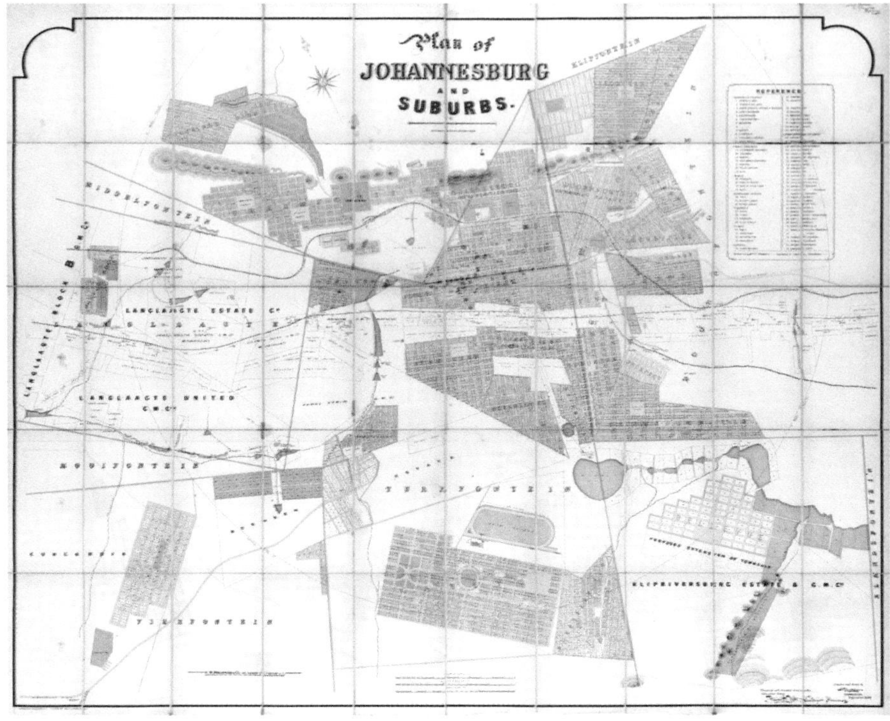

given to the land, streets, suburbs. Four theaters, including the Globe; three newspaper offices; churches of seven denominations; four clubs; hotels; sports facilities; a public park; segregated areas for black laborers, for Indian washer-men, for white mine managers.

But it is also a projection, a wish, a vision of a possible city. At the time the map was drawn and printed, only about 3 percent of the streets and buildings and suburbs on it had been made. It is extraordinary that now, 120 years later, almost all the map exists as physical fact. In the way that a drawing is a membrane between the world coming toward us and our projected understanding of the world, a negotiation between ourselves and that which is outside, this map becomes an emblematic drawing, having as its conscious subject this meeting of the world as it comes to us, and our expanded projection onto it.

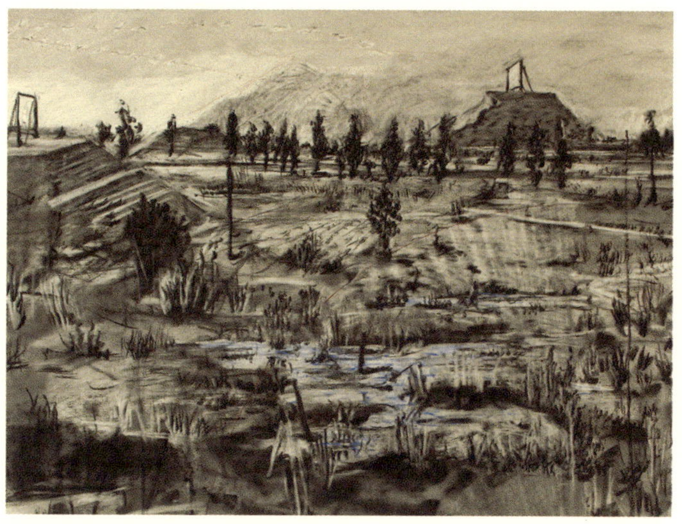

THE LIE OF THE LAND #1

Irrigation of Privilege

Around 1900, at the end of the war between the British and the Afrikaners for control of the gold mines, the city of Johannesburg, wanting to keep the demobilized soldiers busy rather than drunk, employed them at a penny a tree to plant a forest of a million trees on the pavements and in the gardens of the city. Johannesburg, by its own and some outside estimations, is the largest man-made forest in the world. From my studio, you look out over an undulating sea of treetops. The gardens of these leafy suburbs are lush and dense.

The land around and outside Johannesburg is dry, dusty, inhospitable. Scrubby trees and stony ground, thorns, stones, and red dust. The edge of the suburbs marks the end of irrigation and privilege. Water is a charged material here. There is not enough surface water, and water for drinking and industry is pumped from rivers sometimes one hundred kilometers away, sometimes from several hundred kilometers away in Lesotho. The streams of the city itself are miserable ditches, stormwater drains awaiting the rainstorms.

A DROWNING SURFEIT

But underground, where the mining is, it is the reverse. There is too much water. It has to be continually pumped out, it floods the passages and stopes of the mines. The pumping leaves in its wake great sinus cavities in the rock, making the earth vulnerable to collapse. A smooth patch of road suddenly disappears in a sinkhole. In my childhood there were stories of an entire tennis match—the umpire on his high chair, the tea and orange juice on the table next to the court, the family Labrador—all being swallowed by a huge sinkhole, never found, never recovered. Only the tail of a Chevrolet Impala, sticking out of the rubble at the bottom of the hole, a marker of the suburban life gone. This was both a terror in itself, but more than that, an indication of instability. Of a world under the ground.

KNOWN BUT NOT SEEN

The vertical separation, the life above ground and the dark chambers below, had horizontal equivalents. The white areas, the areas outside the city set aside for blacks; separate areas for every group, Indians, mixed-race Coloreds. As a white child I knew they were there, somewhere behind the mine dumps, at the edge of the city, but not seen. The invisibility of the underground had echoes with other things not seen. Of mine compounds, with their rows of concrete bunks, of miners singing underground, of the unstable foundations of these lush gardens and suburban lives.

A geological sense not just of the structure of the city, but of its politics. The rumblings of the earth, the rattling of cups and shelves with earth tremors, as the earth readjusted to its excavations. A message from the dark underground caves, stopes, and passageways of the mines below. Water became both a wish—if only there was water we could have a lush landscape; if only there was a lake, a sea, a shore—and all that went with them. But it also became a drowning threat—with the removal of the water, you could be drowned in the earth itself.

THE LIE OF THE LAND #2

Sighs and Traces

The land is an unreliable witness. It is not that it effaces all history, but events must be excavated, sought after in traces, in half-hidden clues. There is a similarity to the land and what it does, and our unreliable memory. Things which seemed so clear and so embedded in us, fade; a shock, an outrage that we should live by, becomes dull. We have to work to find that first, true impulse. A forest we know contained mass killings is filled with wind in the leaves. Only a section where the trees are shorter, in a straight line, marks the spot of the mass grave. A change of color in the vegetation marks where there were once foundations of a prison block. What should be proclaimed clearly—HERE THIS HAPPENED, let us not forget—becomes ever thinner, ever harder to see, the landscapes and our memory push it farther away, until we get lost in the undergrowth.

Even our outrage is lost. We are left with something closer to regret. Regret at what happened, but also regret at our inability to hold onto our feeling. We are deceived by the landscape. Not only deceived, but disappointed, betrayed. The landscape, and our memory, should be that much stronger.

I remember some years ago taking a train from Munich to Dachau. And the shock of arriving at Dachau station, to see signs inviting to me to Schloss Dachau, to try the wares of the Dachau Konditerei; when to me it seemed the very name itself should have been enough to blast the landscape into barrenness. I had to recalibrate my sense of geography, to change in my head my imagined Dachau to the suburban reality, to the women with shopping bags on their way to the grocery, passing the camp, as they would have in the 1930s and 1940s too.

For the town itself, to understand it was twelve bad years in its 800-year history. But feeling what I lost in the recalibration. Understanding the world as it is, but trying to hold onto that initial impulse, the strength of an emotion clearly felt, laid bare. Finding the traces: the edge of a foundation, the straight lines of the trees. Knowing that when we put up a sign or a label—this event happened in this space, this monument is erected to the memory of—we admit defeat. We hand the responsibility of memory to the sign, to the object. It becomes a canned memory, like canned laughter on a TV show, which laughs on our behalf, it remembers on our behalf, it does the work for us. We are let off the hook.

THERE IS NO GOOD SOLUTION

We need the terrain of the half-solved, the half-solvable riddle, the distance between knowing and not knowing, and being aware of our own limits of understanding, the limits of our memory, but prodding the memory nonetheless.

THE LIE OF THE LAND #3

The Leaf in the Paint
The Stone under the Blanket

When I was nine years old, I went to art lessons. At the first lesson, I was asked by my teacher what I liked to draw. "Landscape," I replied. Where I even knew the word from, I do not know. My grandfather did give me a book, a Hanukkah present, of great landscape paintings of the world, with a landscape with an avenue of trees by Hobbema on the cover; and paintings from Poussin to Constable to Douanier Rousseau—but I think this was years later. "And how do you want to work?" asked the teacher. "Charcoal." Again, I am not sure from where the answer came. I don't think I had ever used it before. But these words, landscape and charcoal, were words I associated with making art. The question is, what kind of landscape does a nine-year-old white Johannesburg boy make?

NOW THIS WAS A LANDSCAPE

Every Friday night, my sister and I had supper with my grandparents in their flat. Over their dining room table hung a large painting by the South African artist Tinus de Jongh. The painting showed a mountain in the background, a river in the foreground, and leafy trees in between. I was struck by how the flecks of yellow paint could become the rocks seen through the tree branches. How horizontal strokes of paint made the surface of the water, how vertical strokes made the reflection in the water—by the transformation of paint into the world, and the world into paint. With your nose against the canvas, it was all paint and brushstrokes; two steps back, and it was illusion. Now this was a landscape: with mountains, shade, color, water. This was the opposite of what we had. No mountains; the grass a parched, desaturated yellow in winter; no rivers, at best a culvert. The landscape and the picturesque were synonymous: they needed a view framed by big trees with layers of foliage, a Baroque theater set of planes of events receding into the distance.

[Show Tinus de Jongh painting.]

WHAT THE WORLD SHOULD BE

It was more than this. This is not just how pictures should be made, what constituted a landscape, but a pattern for the world, an ordered, structured progression moving from the depth of the painting to the foreground of the canvas. This image of the world was in part derived from English children's books. The books in the library, their pictures, their texts, were half of who we were. We deserved what was in them. The dissatisfaction of the landscape reflected a larger dissatisfaction. The world depicted in children's books of villages, vicars, foxes, woods, and streams was all absent. It was our landscape, our lives that were at fault, rather than the fiction. The map could not be completed. The gap between what came up from the world—the barbed-wire fences, the hill with stones and thorns, that we met when the family went out for a picnic outside the city—could not be mapped onto an image of soft grass, rolling hills, spreading trees implied in the blanket and tablecloth that we brought with us to spread out for the picnic. This impasse, this non-meeting of the world, was always expressed in disputes in the car over where we should stop, where we should turn off one dust road onto the next. The sealed seething inside the car was the pressurized point, the center, of this impossibility.

I am not sure what drawing I made, that first lesson, what the landscape was. But I am sure it was neither of barbed wire, nor stones, nor thorns. Only later on, when I came back to draw the landscape around Johannesburg, did it strike me that the drawings started out as revenge. However non- the landscape was, however null, the drawing could track and trace it. However bleak, parched, the view was, it could be put down on paper. However unstructured by the dictates of the picturesque, in the drawing I could record this non-landscape. The drawings became images of traces, of tracts in the landscape, drawings structured by lines and objects, abandoned civil engineering projects, pipes, a culvert.

In the winter of the highveld, there are veld fires, and the yellow grass is reduced to black stubble. It becomes a charcoal drawing in itself. You could drag a piece of paper across the ground, and a charcoal drawing would be made. It is literally the world meeting the drawing halfway, in image, tone, and material. The straight lines on the ground, the power lines, the culverts, the pipes, as straight as the projected vanishing point of a lesson in perspective.

To go back to the nine-year-old at his art lesson, and his landscape: what had he seen, and what could he draw? The landscapes of books, illustrations, and stories; the painting in his grandparents' flat; the reproduction of a Cézanne landscape in his parents' bedroom; the brilliance of sunlight through the fresh spring leaves of the oak trees at his school; the yellow mine dumps at the edge of the city; the stony veld beyond that.

KNOWLEDGE AS SHAME

To pinpoint a Johannesburg childhood more precisely: two things seen, but not spoken of. Driving with his grandfather (who had given him the book of landscape paintings). Passing a side street. A glance. A man lying in the gutter. Four men around him, kicking his body, kicking his head. The shock of adult violence. The nine-year-old knows about kicking someone. But to kick a person in the head, in the face? The world had to rearrange itself, to accommodate this new knowledge. The image was seen, they passed, no mention was made.

When he is six, he goes into his father's study and sees a thin yellow box, which looks like a box of chocolates. The lid is carefully opened. Inside is not the thin wax paper covering the first layer of chocolates, but a sheaf of glossy 10 x 12-inch black and white photographs. A man lies face downward, a dot and a dark stain in the center of his checkered jacket. The next photograph: the man rolled over. An incomprehensible confusion of shirt, jacket, viscera; the whole chest disintegrated by the exit wound of the bullet. The photos continued. A policeman looking down at a woman, arms splayed, shopping bag still in her hand, her head against the pavement curbside. A larger view. People crouching, running toward us, the cameraman. The photograph from behind: people lying spread across the veld. A man sitting dazed, his head in his hands. A policeman standing on top of the armored vehicle. Another chest—is it a man? Is it a woman?—blown apart. The six-year-old closes the box.

Puts it back on the shelf. Puts a book on top of it to hide what he has done. It is more than "this should not happen." THIS SHOULD NOT BE SEEN. He should not have seen it. Not as strong as that his seeing it has made it happen, but a complicity between the event and the sight of it.

These were photographs of the Sharpeville massacres, in 1960, in which sixty-nine black protesters, people protesting the pass laws, were shot in a township outside Vereeniging, a town some fifty miles from Johannesburg. My father was the lawyer representing the families of the people killed, at the inquest held in 1961. The photographs were part of the evidence presented to the court (the court exonerated the policemen). I would have been six years old. I did not ever tell my father that we had both looked at those photographs.

So when I was at the art lesson, this too I had seen—the violence, the bodies in the veld. Not only the Cézanne, the Poussin, the Tinus de Jongh. It was not that the two worlds could not come together, but there was no need for them to: the one was art, the other was life, family, friends, school, the city, the world. There were two parallel streams, one going from Michelangelo's *Last Judgement* (another book from my grandfather) to *The Bar at the Folies Begère*. The other stream was the growing awareness of the unnaturalness of Johannesburg life. The faultline glimpsed. The sinkhole in Carletonville, the man in the gutter, the bullet wounds in the photographs.

IN PRAISE OF BASTARDY

Instruction Manuals Absent

There are no long local traditions in Johannesburg, only that which has been imported and constructed. Traditions imported, still in their boxes. First English, Cornish miners; then Chinese indentured miners; African miners from Mozambique, Nyasaland, different corners of South Africa. Following the pogroms of the 1880s, Jews fled Lithuania. Many, including my family, settled in South Africa, and after the discovery of gold made their way to Johannesburg.

Traders came from Gujarat in India. It is not that there was an easy mixing, a soup of nations. Of course, Jews largely met with Jews, Indians from Gujarat largely met with Indians from Gujarat, Mozambicans met with Mozambicans. But there were points of intersection. The weight of a single, central tradition was less. Even the weight of Europe, hanging over the heads of schoolchildren and students in the city, was understood in a colonial way—believing we misunderstood the great texts, that only in Europe could Plato be understood—but reconstructing them as best we could, AS IF this is what the texts, the traditions, could have meant. The productive misunderstanding and mistranslation were both essential. The sense of being at the edge of tradition, at the corner of the great works, both instilled a colonial fear of misunderstanding, of being less smart, less wise, than those in the centers, Europe and the United States, and also made for freedom in the leaps that had to be made, the leaps of what a text could or might mean, or AS IF they meant X or Y. Filling in the sections which we assumed we did not understand.

BROKEN REPORTS

In the studio, this becomes an improvisation with traditions, a collage of fragments of different modernisms. Distant dispatches of what happened in the center reached us—a real pump, pumping real honey though a building. A pile of bricks in a museum. A student protest now called public sculpture. None of this was familiar or comprehensible. All was there to be used—possible meanings we would construct for ourselves. A do-it-yourself improvisation of meaning.

SECOND CITIZEN

The second most illustrious citizen of the city came to South Africa as a young lawyer. He was from a high-caste Hindi family. Gandhi arrived to look after the legal interests of Indian traders. He was not interested in Indian mysticism, had no knowledge of Sanskrit. Gandhi's transformation, during the twenty years he was in Johannesburg, came through several sources. First, it came through his observation of a Muslim passive protest, of Muslim activists who urged Indians to go to jail rather than obey oppressive new restrictive laws. Second, it came through contact with a group of Jewish intellectuals and architects, who gave him John Ruskin's *Unto This Last* to read, and who introduced him to Indian mysticism—and this through theosophy, the construction of a Russian Madame Blavatsky and her American colleague, Henry Steel Olcott. This mysticism was a mixture of Victorian talking to the dead and a version of the spirituality of Hinduism and Buddhism.

Through this Russian, American, English, German-Jewish mixture, Gandhi came to read the Bhagavad Gita. He came back to his tradition, to rethinking his political philosophy, while in detention in the fort in Johannesburg in 1908. It was here that he developed his philosophy and politics of Satyagraha. He was not a scholar of Indian philosophy. His education had been outside that tradition. He was a smartly dressed English barrister. When he came back to his tradition, it was through this mistranslation, through the use and misuse to which the texts had been subject. The tradition bastardized, approached from the side, not to continue it, or pay homage to it, but to use it as raw material in the service of another end.

It is a city of possible transformations. Gandhi could escape his caste position and make connections and political leaps that would have been impossible in India.

DELIGHT IN THE INCOHERENCE

The city and the studio meet in the form of collage, of disintegration, in the reconstructability of physical space, of the space of thought, in the making and unmaking of images in the studio. There is not a script or a storyboard. There is a contingency to meaning and what can be gleaned from fragments coming together. A construction rather than a discovery. As with a drawing, a meeting of the world halfway. Only in retrospect does anything have determined inevitability.

FIXED ASSETS / PORTABLE PROPERTY

There is a provisionality at the heart of the city. Not just a provisionality of architecture—of theaters, houses, offices built with the confidence of surviving centuries, only for them to be imploded to make way for new developments each time the economy boomed. The beautiful Art Deco buildings in the center of town demolished in the great boom of the 1960s, the economic boom coinciding with the most brutal, narrow period of apartheid oppression. The provisionality goes further than the city to the landscape itself.

Hills and mountains are markers of solidity: a rock the symbol of eternity, a mountain a symbol of that which cannot be moved. A mountain is a fact, a fixed object in a shifting world, against which we can measure ourselves. The hills of the city of Johannesburg are a low series of ridges south of the city center. Yellow, flat-topped mountains, made from the earth and rock excavated from the mines. Some grassed over, some still the yellow of the cyanide-treated crushed earth. Traces of danger, both from the cyanide and from the threat of the friable earth collapsing. Children playing on the mine dumps would be drowned by landslides. The wastelands between the dumps had their own dangers: unmarked, abandoned mine shafts, waiting to swallow anyone; stories of thieves and highwaymen hiding in the scrubland. But they were our hills, our mountains. Seen at the end of the streets in the city, the flat tops a reassuring view as one returned from holiday.

Then metallurgical techniques changed. It became possible to extract the fine residue of gold dust that remained in these dumps. The price of gold went up, and the hills started disappearing. Another legal note: there was a dispute over these hills. Were they the fixed property of the people who owned the land? Or moveable assets that were owned by the original miners, for them to be removed, re-processed, and abandoned somewhere else? While this case was still proceeding through the courts, trucks and high-pressure hoses arrived at night, and the hills were erased. A drive-in cinema perched on the top of one of these hills, the TopStar, was a heritage site, but the hill underneath it was not. The hill was successively eaten away from around it. The screen was finally dismantled a year ago.

The city becomes its own large-scale animated drawing, erasing and redrawing itself. As the dumps disappear, there is a first moment of shock at the reconfiguration of the landscape; and then a naturalization of the view, as if the mine dump had never been there. This adaptability is more than the flexibility to accept a new situation. It is stronger than that. You cannot remember what it looked like before, what the mine dump looked like. And the accompanying regret is also a regret at our ease of forgetting. You have to look at a photograph to see the dump again, to remember, to say, "Oh yes, that is what it was like in the olden days"—even if the olden days were only six months ago. The photograph, like the label on the monument, like the monument itself, has to stand in for memory. The city becomes an object lesson in provisionality, not just in the matter of structure and mountains, but of memory itself.

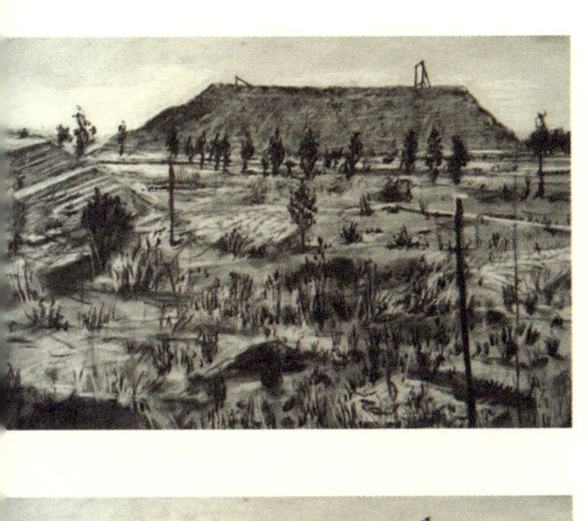
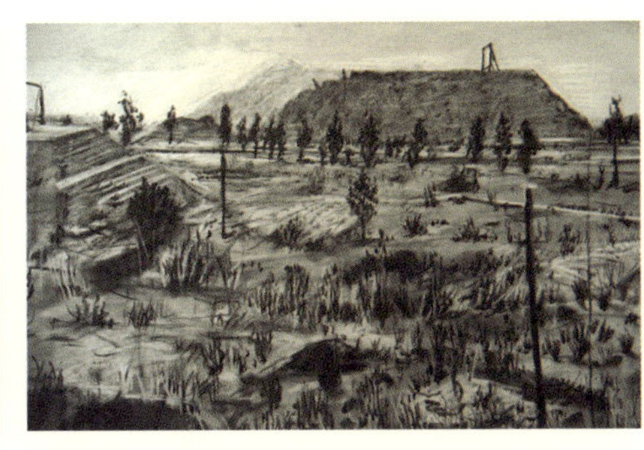
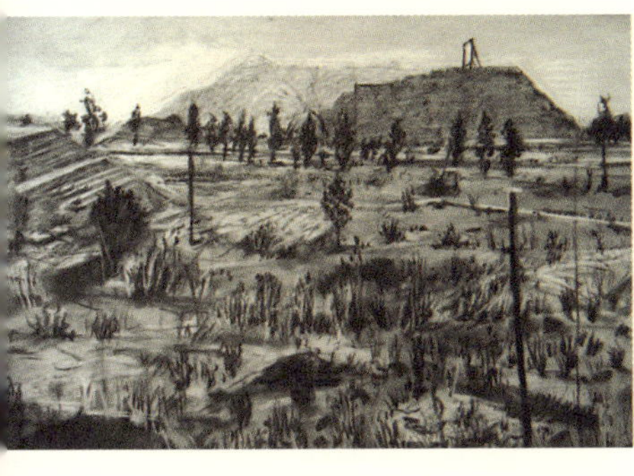
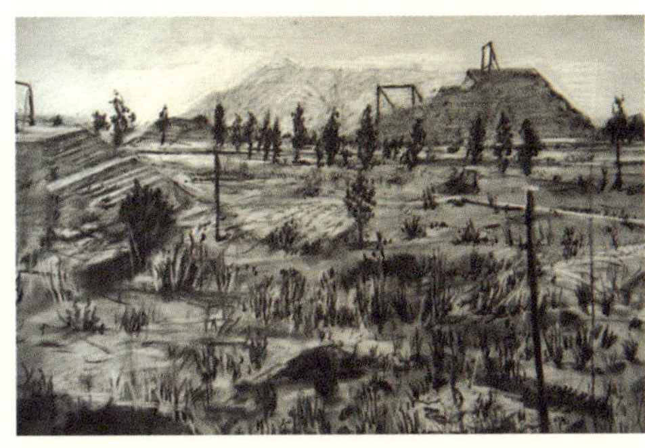
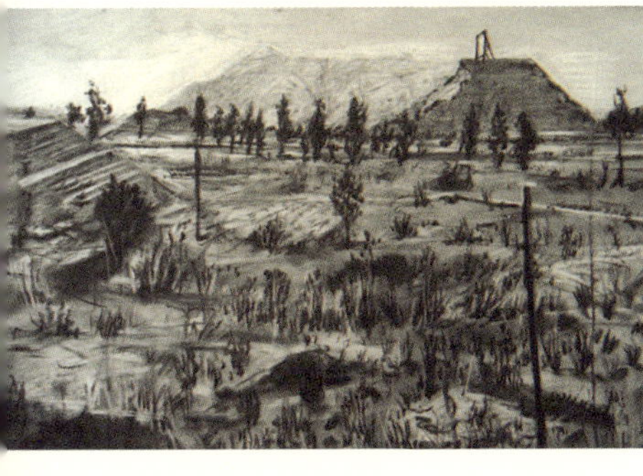
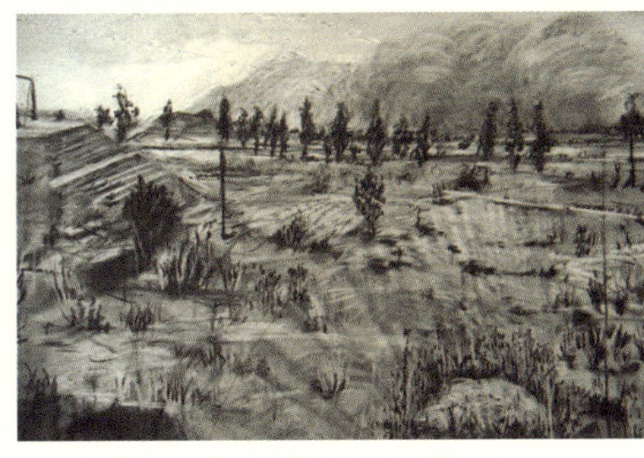

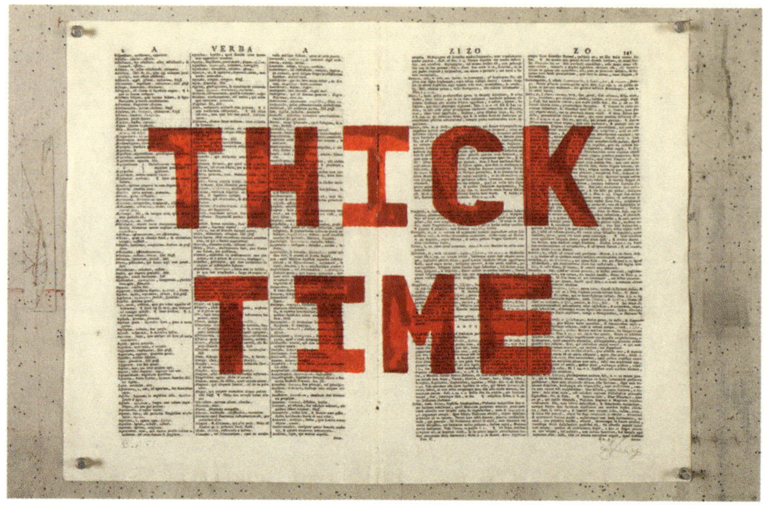

THICK TIME

[Show studio filming and drawing,
the walk to and from the camera.]

To leave the southern edge of the city, and come four kilometers north, to the studio, and to the technology of trying to track these processes. A sheet of paper on the wall of the studio. A camera in the center of the room. A walk between the camera and the wall. Altering the drawing, walking to the camera, recording the alteration. The studio becomes a machine for the alteration of time.

First in the most crass sense: time becomes distance, it becomes matter, it expands and contracts, it becomes visible. Time becomes distance twice. A film camera is a device for turning time into calculable distance. In traditional film projection, twenty-four frames of film pass between the lamp and the lens every second. The twenty-four frames of 35mm film are eighteen inches in length, or 45.5 centimeters. Time gets turned into distance and numbers of frames. Fifteen hundred frames a minute. Seven hundred and fifty alterations to a drawing, if one is filming two frames per alteration. The invisible substance of

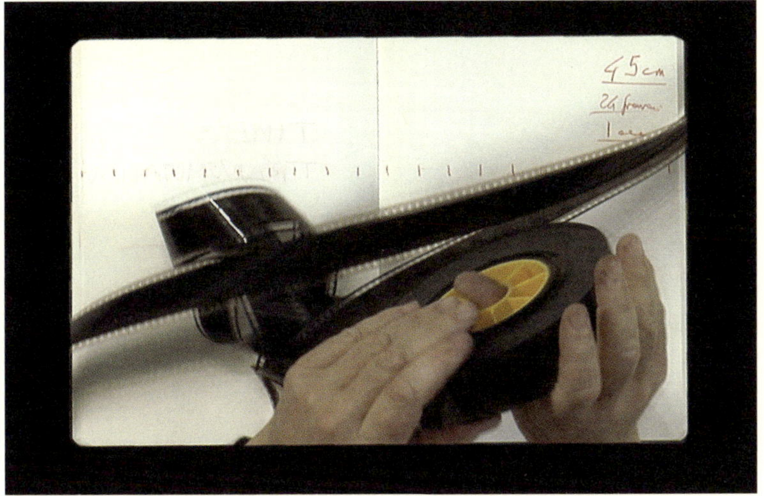

time gets turned into the material of film. The ribbon of film both holds and calibrates time. Holding the discus-like roll of film, one is also holding duration. Other objects of course also embody time. An oak tree holds in its trunk two centuries of growing. But the roll of film holds as its essence the materialization of time.

TIME FORGOTTEN

[Show drawing an arc, animating it.]

Across the studio, in the notebook, time becomes distance again. I make a sweep of my wrist and trace an arc on the sheet of paper. It takes one and a half seconds for the sweep. One and a half seconds is thirty-six frames. I divide the line of the arc into thirty-five divisions, and draw and film each division successively: drawing a mark, walking to the camera, filming, walking back to the drawing, making the next mark. In the camera, the record of time becomes twenty-seven inches of film. On the paper, the thirty centimeter sweep of the arm becomes a series of eight millimeter divisions of charcoal marks. The focus shifts

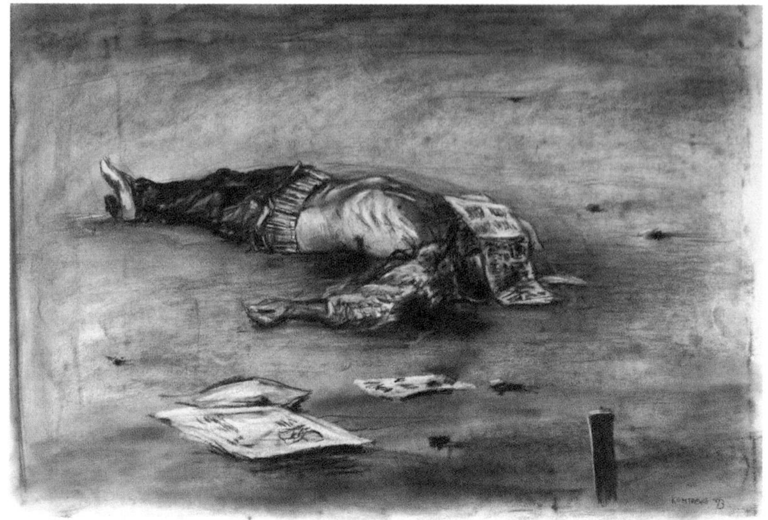

entirely to the divisions, the marks—successively joining them up. Time is forgotten in the activity of drawing time. Each mark on the paper is a record of the move between the camera and the paper, the passage of time, and becomes an ink line.

Of course, what still stays invisible is the passage of time in the making of the image of time. The twenty minutes to make the one and a half seconds. The year to make a ten-minute film. This change of a line, of a gesture, into discrete marks, stands in for a larger change. The central inversion in the studio, like the inversion of light as it passes through the pinhole of the aperture of a camera. On one side of the aperture is the world, events, history, the family picnics, the Sharpeville photos, the Sharpeville massacre itself. On the other side of the aperture it is transformed. It is not that the events, history, disappear, but they are changed, into a series of discrete marks. The world is unmade, to be made again.

Drawing a body in the veld. I start with a reference for the drawing, a photograph of a body. A police photograph, not the Sharpeville photographs, though it could have been. The drawing was made for a film with bodies in the veld. Only after the drawing was finished did I remember the Sharpeville photographs. I remembered what I had been drawing, long after the drawing was finished.

FINDING THE IMAGE

The activity of drawing itself. The concentration shifts position. The image becomes a series of marks and decisions. The person shot, the provoking shot, disintegrates into the tone, the line, the contrast of the drawing. Over the paper hovers a projection of the figure, but overlaying it too are all the other bodies: Goya's spread-eagled man from *The Third of May;* Giotto's *Massacre of the Innocents;* the flayed skin of Marseus. But then they too are too far from the paper. Right up against the paper, the activity of finding the image is just the material and the belief that this material will transform itself back into the image—the darkness of the line, the texture of the paper, white pastel over an erased gray. Following the shifts and decisions as one would follow the divisions of the line divided into its thirty-seven sections. Understanding that the cumulative work, the labor power expended, together with the belief in the activity, will make the image emerge.

Right up against the paper, a still life by Chardin or Morandi is as good a guide as any. Anger, distress, desire may have been behind the impulse to make the image, but here they are left behind. Time slows down and becomes outside the image. Something glimpsed for a second may take a day, or days, to draw. Pleasure, frustration, self-doubt, states evoked by the materials and activity, take the place of the initial impulse. There is still some connection to the first thought; but it is on hold. The impulse is sent to wait outside in an antechamber while the work is being done.

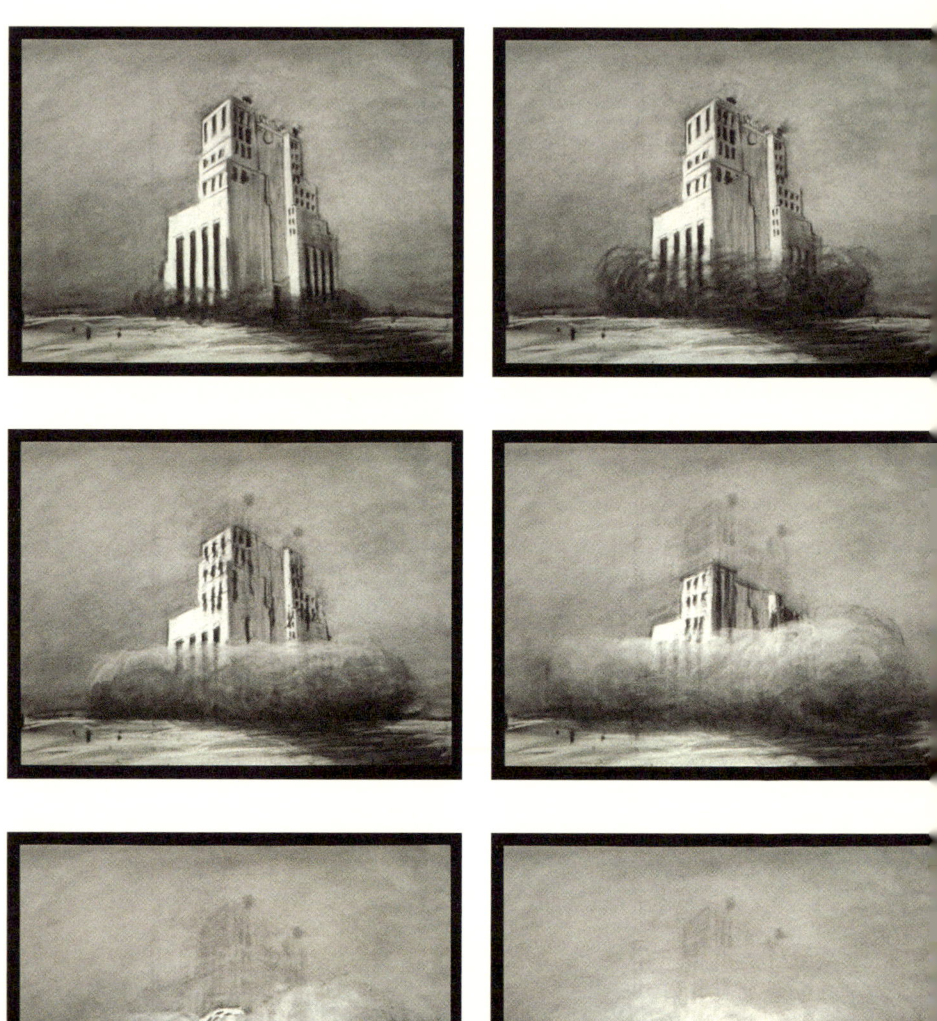

IMPERFECT ERASURE

There are other ways in which time becomes thickened with material. Charcoal and paper are not perfect substances. Charcoal can be erased easily, but not perfectly. The paper is tough and can be erased, redrawn, erased, and still hold its structure—but not without showing its damage. The erasure is never perfect. A gray smudge of charcoal dust lodged in the paper fibers remains as the ghost of the image before its alteration. In the camera, the film records the alteration, and the ghost of the history of alteration: they are embedded in the camera. Time gets transformed into the charcoal dust, the damaged fibers of the paper, the flecks of plastic eraser clinging to the surface of the drawing. The hill is neither there, still, as in the photograph, in which it is seen as it will always be seen; nor is it entirely absent, as it is in our memories, where we have naturalized its absence. It hovers in the smudges on the paper and in the roll of film in the camera, awaiting processing and projecting.

A DAILY CONSTITUTIONAL

The provisionality, the uncertainty, the instability, is lodged in the materials, their technique, and the technology itself. The imperfect erasure is not an artifact, an effect added. It is what the making, the physical activity—the drawing, the erasing, the filming, the walking—throws toward us. The studio meeting the world halfway. The walk is vital, not just in how it echoes the other walking in the studio, the walk of waiting for ideas to emerge and gather themselves; but in a separation between the making and the looking. There is the drawing that happens, standing close to the paper, where all becomes lines of charcoal, the marks of the eraser, the wipe of the chamois cloth. The walk back to the camera, or back to the drawing, is a re-imagining of how the drawing could look. The turn to shoot the next frame,

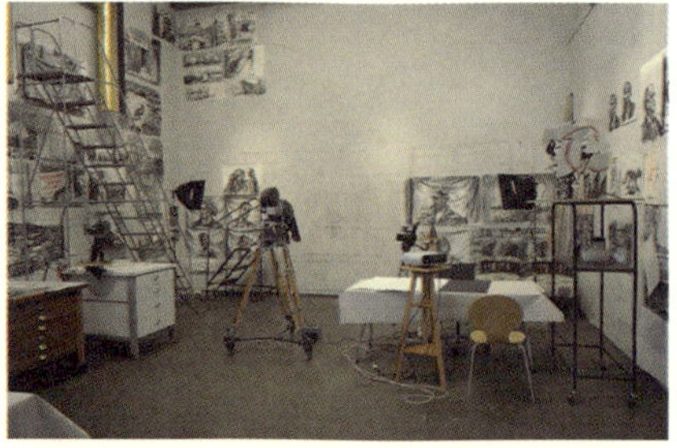
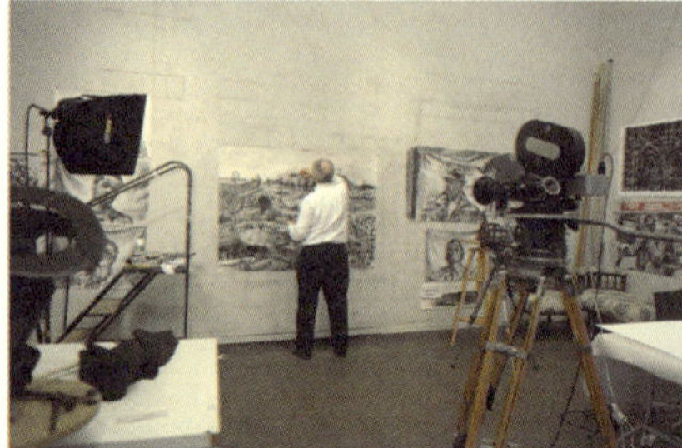
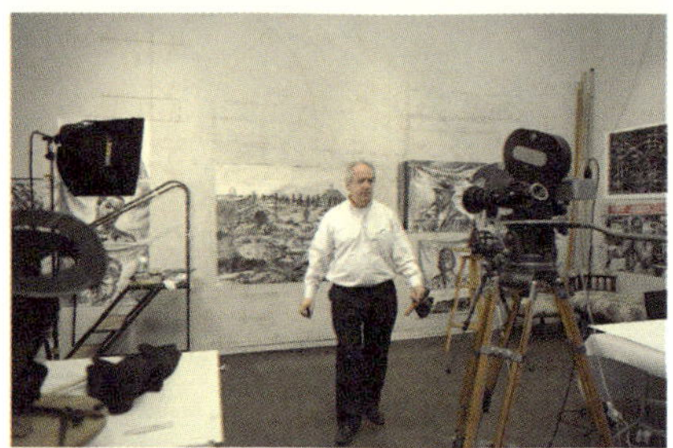
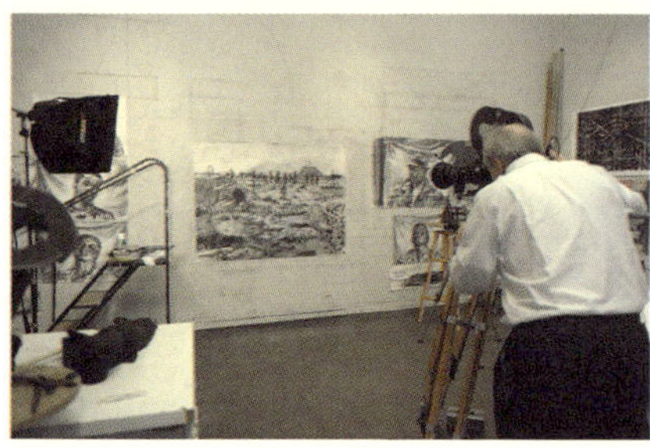
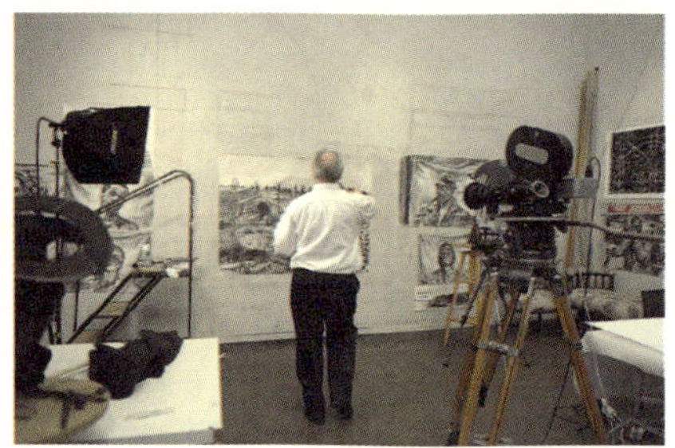
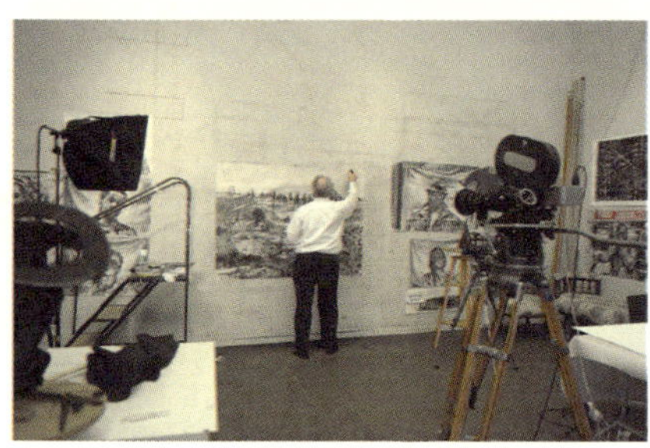

the glance, the fresh glance at the drawing on the turn, where the artist as viewer judges, instructs, castigates, or gives a nod of "just carry on."

VERTICAL THINKING

The city remaking itself is an essentially vertical phenomenon. Buildings, the mountain, are brought down to ground level, and new structures rise up. This is not a lateral pan, along the horizon line, taking in an expanse of landscape; it is not extent, not a Cinemascope sweep, but a rising and falling in front of us.

Like the roll of film passing through the gate of the camera. The film, having a glimpse of the world of light and shade, as each frame is held steady, given a glimpse of this outside world, and then sent down into the dark cave of the take-up spool. As if the film itself could penetrate the earth, go past the cave of the early hominids, still farther down to the stopes and passages of miners underground, to the geological time of the meteor impact.

As if the whole universe could swirl down, from its largest sources, from the origin of the meteor, down to that specific, exact place, passing through the eye of the needle, through the aperture of the camera. Holding on, showing this compression of time, holding this time in the material roll of celluloid.

DIALECTICS FOR NINE-YEAR-OLDS

I have described Johannesburg as a city with a lack of geography: no rivers, no seashore, no geographic *raison d'être*. Apart from the gardens, we are outside of nature. But there is one category in which we still hang on. We have our local sublime. Not the stormy oceans, or the mighty Alps, or glaciers of the traditional sublime, in which the human is so dwarfed by the scale of natural phenomena that we feel our insignificance and how small we are against the horizon of time and the world—and we revel in this revelation.

In Johannesburg, we have dry winters. In summer we have heat, and thunderstorms in the afternoons. Our sublime arrives in the form of huge cumulus nimbus clouds that pile themselves up over the city. With every day, when we have a storm, a new mountain range, a new Alps, is built for us again. In the way that the mine dumps can exist, be erased, be rebuilt, so from a clear sky the cathedrals of clouds construct themselves. We see two things in the clouds. Shapes: a dog's head, an old man's face with a protruding chin; the back of a head on a shoulder. This is not about our ability to see things. It is not an act of generosity to see them. It is about not being able to stop ourselves from seeing the shapes. The man's head comes to you. Once recognized, you cannot stop yourself from seeing it. This is one element of the clouds. The other is the changing itself, the shifting form of them, an awareness of the engine in the clouds, a force changing the form and the shape.

Lying on one's back, looking at the clouds in the late afternoon, there is a seed of understanding that a child gets, of the nature of provisionality, of the indwelling tendency outward: the tendency that sits inside something, that moves to emerge. Something is growing within, changing the outside form, becoming itself.

I think of myself as a nine-year-old looking at the clouds. And I think of myself as that nine-year-old still stuck inside the frame of this fifty-six-year-old. I feel his anxiety as he runs around inside me still. The nine-year-old is saying, "Tell them about this. Tell them about . . . Tell them about the landscape, that I worked hard, that I wanted to make my mother happy." He gets more and more agitated, the nine-year-old inside. Then the thunder comes, and huge drops of rain. I say to the nine-year-old, "It's all right, it's all right. You don't have to run so hard."

END DRAWING LESSON THREE

Drawing Lesson Four

PRACTICAL EPISTEMOLOGY: LIFE IN THE STUDIO

A HISTORY OF CINEMA #1

In the autumn of 1786, an English designer of theatrical sets, Philip James de Loutherbourg, opened a theater in London in Drury Lane, the Eidophusikon, in which the only performers were the painted sets themselves. With gauzes, scrims, and changing lights, a series of different scenic effects would be shown: the eruption of Mount Vesuvius; sunset over Naples; a candle-lit palace at Versailles; the destruction of Gomorrah. People would come to sit in the darkened theater to watch these metamorphoses.

Cinema can be described as a continuation of these performances of transformation. The nineteenth century had a series of such performances, usually seen in variety theater and vaudeville shows.

There was shadowgraphy, in which the performers would make different shadows with their hands—a rabbit, a butterfly, the old woman with a hooked nose and protruding chin (index and baby finger, right hand, essential here; left hand to make her hat). The shadows would be worked into a story—but what held the audience's attention, of course, was the double play of hand into shadow; the movement of the hands, the changes of one shadow into the next.

There was chapeauism, in which a performer would take a felt hat, and with a twist or a flip, turn the hat into a fisherman's cap, Napoleon's tricorn, a bonnet. Malleability of material—the felt rag—and the skill of the performer were the subjects here.

There were quick-change artists: an empty stage with a

screen. The performer on one side of the stage, dressed as a dandy; he crosses behind the screen and emerges as a tramp. The transformation of clothes and character faster than seemed possible.

And stage magicians, who could combine the speed of hand, the practiced skill of the shadow artist, with the mechanical illusions of the Eidophusikon to make objects appear, disappear, and change. A handkerchief into a dove, a rabbit into a bunch of roses. These performers were working both with and against time. The Eidophusikon speeding up time, the sunset over Capri condensed from its one and a half hours into two minutes. Spinning the world faster on its axis.

The stage magician works with the time of the audience. A hand drops a glove into a hat, and in the same rhythm pulls out a goose. Inside the hat, everything is speeded up. A trapdoor opens, the gloves are tucked away, the goose's neck found and pulled through the trapdoor, the trapdoor and false top of the hat closed. Making that which is fast and frantic appear slow and relaxed. The separation between the frenzied working of the right hand in the hat, and the casually gesturing left hand.

In the late 1890s, Georges Méliès, one such stage magician, started using short films in his performances. These were initially simply one more performance of transformation. The most complicated changes, disappearances, changes in scale, disembodiments, could be accelerated by simply stopping time, adjusting the world, and allowing time to continue. An action could be filmed. The camera and the action halted at the crucial moment (the stage assistant passing behind the screen), an

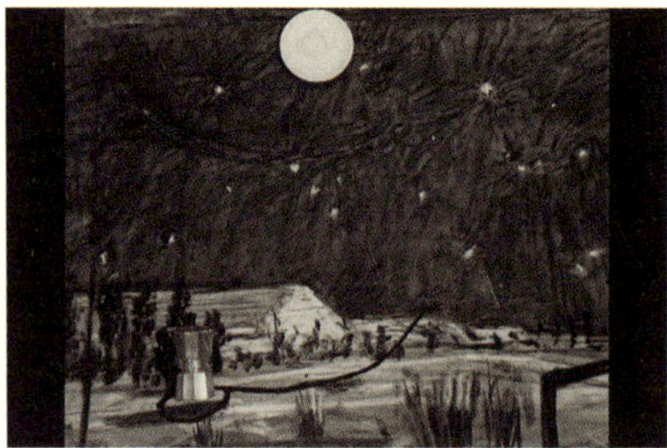

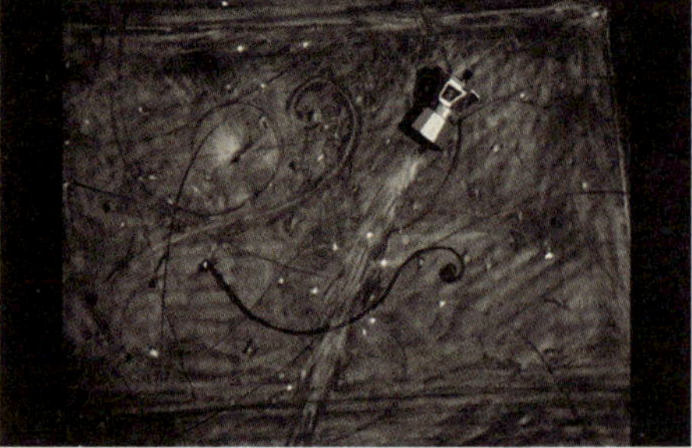

alteration to the world made—the change of costume that could be both leisurely and elaborate—and then the action and the camera continuing (the transformed assistant now exits from behind the screen, accompanied by six lions). When projected, the period out of time was invisible, the transformation seamless.

Most of the 500 films that Méliès made in the first two years of working with film were explorations. More than explorations, celebrations of these skills, these possibilities of a new way the world could be imagined in the studio. I will show you a man who can take his head off and put it under his arm. Playing cards that can come alive. A head that can be inflated like a beach ball. A suitcase that contains not just a piano but a whole room of furniture—not only that, but a family to occupy the room and eat the food at the dining room table. And then put them all back in the suitcase, only the empty wine bottles in Méliès's studio left to prove that it actually happened.

To locate where we are: we have come from Plato's cave in lecture one, to the colonies of Africa in lecture two, down to Johannesburg in lecture three, and now we are in the studio. We continue the questions raised in the first lecture on shadows and the agency of seeing.

I have referred to the cinema of Georges Méliès. Again I would like to start with a studio film against which to set the reflections that follow. The film we will look at is my version of Georges Méliès's film *Journey to the Moon*. The film is six and a half minutes long.

[Show film *Journey to the Moon*.]

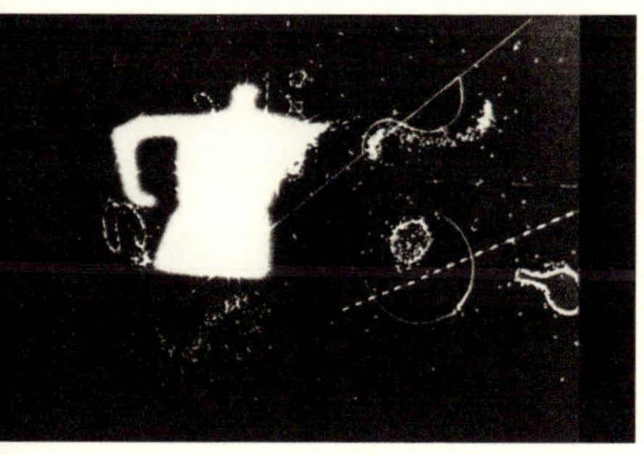

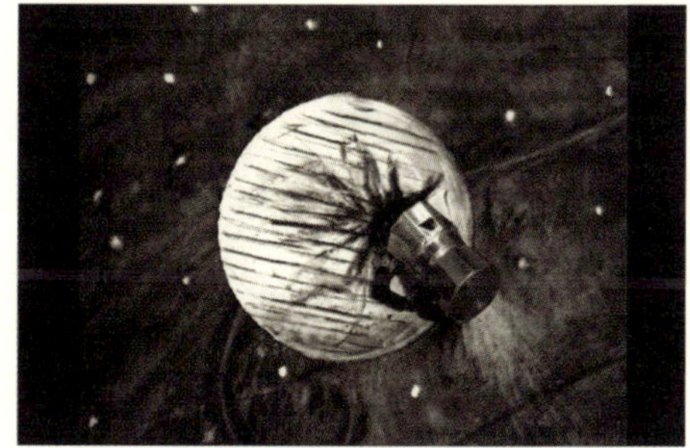

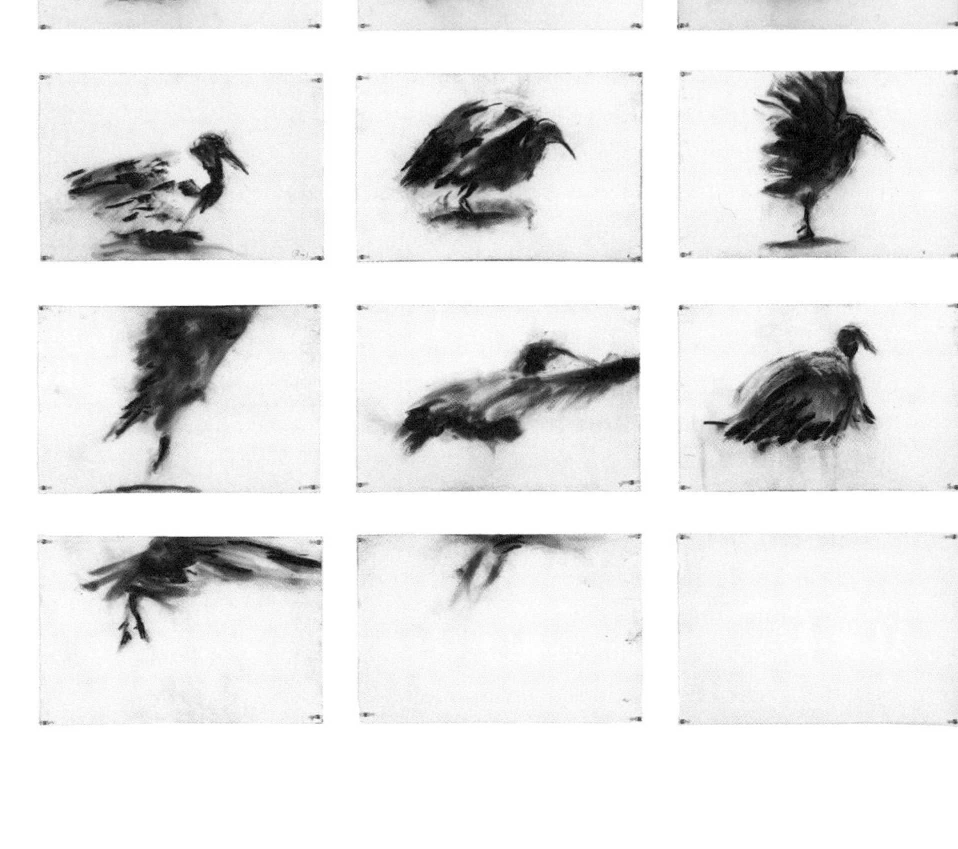

A HISTORY OF CINEMA #2: TIME INTO STONE

The mid-nineteenth-century invention of photography turned time into stone. The first steps of photography relied on fixed, unmoving elements. Slow chemicals meant slow exposures. The camera had to hold something in its gaze for minutes for it to be imprinted on the silver-coated glass. Rocks, buildings, streets could be congealed. Objects in movement could best be detected as ghosts, disturbances in the solid objects behind them. Only the unmoving shoe-polisher and his client, or a man asleep on a city bench, could force their way onto the glass. An image had to sediment itself until the picture was thick with time. Portraits were made with the sitter's head in a clamp, a restraint to keep the head still. Not so that the subject would be forced to see the shadows on the cave wall, but so that the chemical fossilization of the image on the film could happen, and the plate slowly absorb that which was in front of it.

The development of moving photography, of the cinema, at the end of the century made an examination of this congealed time possible. That which was past could be made to pass again. A roll of film could be looked at again and again. More than that, the strip of film with a string of successive images could be looked at backward: time could be held to account.

I film the flight of a bird. I reverse the projection and follow the flight to its origins in the first spring of legs and awkward spread of wings. The destination of an action can be chased back to its first impulse. The history could be contained in a roll of film ready to be reeled in, called back, re-examined. An action done can be undone. A tear forward becomes a repair backward. You can make a palindrome of an action and its anti-action. An action half-completed, half-repeated. We make Rorschach blots of intentions half-made and half-withdrawn. I start to say something, and call the words back.

[WK performs actions and words forward and in reverse.]

AS IF I COULD / DUK I FI SA
AS IF I COULD SWALLOW / OLLAWS DUK I FI SA
AS IF COULD SWALLOW WHAT I HAD JUST SAID
/ DES TSUJ DA I
TOH OLLAWS DUK I FI SA
TNEM I TOH TON STAH / THAT'S NOT WHAT I
MEANT
LOH TA TNEM I TOH TON STAH / THAT'S NOT
WHAT I MEANT AT ALL

MY EIGHT-YEAR-OLD SON

In the studio, I film my eight-year-old son. He takes a jar of paint and a handful of pencils, some books and papers. He throws the jar of paint across the studio walls, scatters the pencils, tears the papers and scatters the shards. We run the film in reverse. There is a utopian perfection. The papers reconstruct themselves perfectly every time. He gathers them all. He catches twelve pencils, all arriving from different corners of the room in the same moment. In the jar he catches all the paint—not a drop is spilled. The wall is pristine.

His joy at his own skill is overflowing. "Can I do it again?" he asks. Yes. But first we have to clean the studio, clean the paint off the wall, pick up the torn paper, gather the pencils. His delight in discovering his own power to remake the world—he was much more than he knew, or that he appeared to be. At any rate, it was discovery of prowess, not a demonstration of it. The film revealed to him things about himself and the world, rather than simply demonstrating something he already knew.

This giving over to the medium is crucial. Allowing a space for the medium to lead, giving yourself over to the play itself. Playing not in the sense of following rules known in advance, as in sport; but play in the sense of the play of light on water.

Not a random activity, but giving yourself over to what the activity provokes, and then following these possibilities assiduously, as you would follow the irrational rules of any game. Irrational, ad hoc constraints followed rigorously. Following the metaphor back to the surface, rather than going from sense and hunting for a metaphor. Discovering the utopian impulse of reversals is a starting point. The following of the provocation, the discovering of the rules of that game, the mastery of it, is a separate activity.

I walk backward, and film myself walking backward, so I can project it forward. It is clearly wrong. The lean is in the wrong direction. I have to lean against the walk, leaning forward when walking backward—the equivalent of leaning backward when walking forward—it is against the natural position where your weight should be. I lean forward as I walk backward, an unnatural action, to make a natural illusion.

This is the work of the studio. The constant filming, performing, reviewing, rewinding, checking; trying to learn how to achieve a reversal that seems a natural forward movement. Walking and filming, leaning at different angles, watching the film back, seeing how one can pause and advance. A series of slow-motion dances without any purpose.

I take a book and throw the book. Do I pause before the throw? Or after the throw? So that when the book returns, I am anticipating it, or it arrives of its own accord? Again, the book-throwing has to be done many times in different ways; this is the engine of the studio work. A series of irrational activities, ad hoc decisions, followed with as much assiduity as possible. Trying to find from the action, from the repetition of the action, the rules of the game and how best to play it.

There seem to be three elements here: something to be seen, the filming of the boy in reverse, number one. The metaphoric suggestions from this, the utopian perfectability of the world in reverse, number two. And the learning of this grammar, how to perform these actions, how to complete and enlarge on the possibilities shown, number three. The idea is never enough. It is how it is achieved. The rehearsal, the filming and refilming, the repeated activities. Learning how to film the final shot. This is a process of making and looking.

Now a fourth thing appears. Remember, we have gone from the outside event, the first proposition, the filmed action looked at backward; to the metaphorical suggestion that emerges from watching what we have filmed—the world is perfectible; to the practical studying, repeat filming, rehearsing, learning the grammar needed to perform the metaphor—how to walk backward, where to pause in throwing the pencils; and the fourth thing that happens, during the learning of the grammar, is the new set of possibilities that emerge while performing the repeated actions—the expansion of the ideas. Walking backward can become catching books backward, to writing backward. Imagine a page of text sucked back into the pen, until the embroidery of the page is all inside the fat tube of the pen, snug in the hand, and all the text becomes potentiality again. This potentiality and its loss become a further theme.

LEAP BEFORE YOU LOOK

We are talking about a trust placed in the physical. That is, through the physical materials and techniques—drawing, filming, walking—new thoughts, new images, will arise. Being led by the body, rather than simply the mind ordering the body about. Not random action, but action, rehearsal, performance, prompted or demanded by the discipline itself. We look at something usually taken for granted, the passage of time, the movement of a person, and in the studio we demand its reconstruction, its shattering. Time changed into the marked graduations of animation: learning its grammar in the hope that in the end something different will emerge. The same happens in performance. The movement of the body, the backward and forward walking, allowing it space, time to show us something unpredicted, unanticipated.

[WK performs the different degrees of tension.]

Here are six different degrees of tension in a body. They can be schematized in text, but they need to be performed for their veracity to be felt.

WK performs level 1

The first degree of tension, level 1: no tension. The minimum needed not to collapse, not to die. There is a breath and a voice that goes with it, though difficult to discern, difficult to hear. A person dying of thirst at the edge of a desert [demonstrate].

WK back to normal (level 4)

This is an exercise from theater school. I last rehearsed it in 1981. We take our chances.

WK performs level 2

A second degree of tension, level 2: complete relaxation, looseness in limbs, in the pelvis, an easy breath, a relaxed walk, a very casual way of talking, intimate. The *flaneur*.

WK back to normal (level 4)

When working on a performance, we can begin with an analysis of the text, a rational dissection of motives, a pre-history of a character, the literary references. Or we can start from the practical, the physical.

WK performs level 3

A third degree of tension, level 3: neutral. An action is done. I walk across the room. I turn the page of my notebook. I breathe. I talk. I say the words that need to be said.

WK goes through the levels 1–4

So here we have gone from level 1, which is relaxed, which is easy, as you can see, to level 3. These are specific, learnable changes of gear. Learning them is like learning the grammar of rehearsals. They need to be performed, the body needs to feel them in the muscles.

WK performs level 4

Level 4. We have more tension. We have purpose and impulse. I cross the stage because I want to cross the stage. I want to make this clear. Can you hear the difference in voice? A connection should be made. We are getting to the heart of the matter. Listen. I want you to follow.

WK playing across all levels

To recapitulate: level 1, OK. Level 2 is familiar now, wada wada wada (we all die anyway). Relax, no problem. Person asleep in row three, that's fine. I continue. We are in level 3. There is no emotion, there are facts. There are propositions, $x + y = 27$. To change to where I want to explain, level 4, I want to say that x is usually 9, y is usually 11.

That here, in level 4, we have impulse, a push behind the movement. A belief that through the action, there are things one can learn.

To go to level 5, where, you MUST understand, it is NOT an action against PSYCHOLOGY; I LOVE psychology. You can see the TENSION in your DESIRE, the ANGLED LIMBS of COMMEDIA DELL'ARTE, the BIG GESTURES, the FULL EMOTIONS of melodrama; all impulses FULLY EXPRESSED.

WK back to normal (level 4)

But where are we going now, in the argument? Where we are going now in this argument is finding the connection, the connection that can come from leading the brain, the body going to the brain, reversing and breaking the blood-brain barrier.

WK performs levels as called for

Come out of level 3, Plato. Inevitably, it is so. Yes, I agree, it is as you say. It cannot be otherwise.

This is a stupid exercise—I am now in level 4, to calibrate ourselves;

this is foolish—level 3;

whatever—level 2;

this is NONSENSE, a pack of LIES, from A to Z!—level 5.

But to get to sense, we first have to go through nonsense—level 4.

LEVEL 5, to shake us OUT of COMPLACENCY,

to shake us out of complicity—level 3.

Level 3, this is not about knowing in advance,

level 4, but recognizing it when we see it. But we are in level 4.

[End of performance of degrees of tension in the body.]

This is a stupid exercise, done in rehearsals with actors, or with drawing students, to show how the body can lead the thought. There is a level 6, reaching a maximum of tension, corresponding to the performers in Noh theater, where there is so much tension, there is virtually no movement, no voice, a F R E E E E E Z E of thinking.

In theatrical terms, this is a way of arriving at a character, finding the psychology from the movement, the breath, the voice. A way of generating not just a performance, but an interaction. Place an actor who will not leave level 3 with someone in level 5, and instantly you have comedy. Make one character shift instantly between level 5 and level 2, and you have a dog-loving demagogue. Not just the great dictator of Chaplin, but the great dictator of the films of Hitler himself. Stalin's voice in recordings always seems set at the relaxed level 2, all the more terrifying for the gap between the gentleness of tone and the action behind the sweetness.

Where are we, at this point? In the studio, with a camera, a roll of film, a performer. Starting with the camera, looking at the roll of film that has been made—the performer playing the scales of levels of tension, the world running backward. And looking outside the camera, at what things these images, this action, provokes. Looking at the change from physical action into thought. At this point of transfer, where through a kind of reverse osmosis, the action is impulse to the thought.

HISTORY OF CINEMA #3

There is another history of cinema, which can be written in terms of technologies of looking. Let us look at five such technologies in the studio: the stereoscope; the phenakistoscope, or all types of zoetropes; the anamorphic mirror; the Claude glass; and the etching press. Each of these is a pre-cinematic device, which takes an element of how we see, removes it from the world of naturalized, invisible vision, turning it into a material object, producing at the end a reconfigured seeing, changing both our sense of the world and our sense of self.

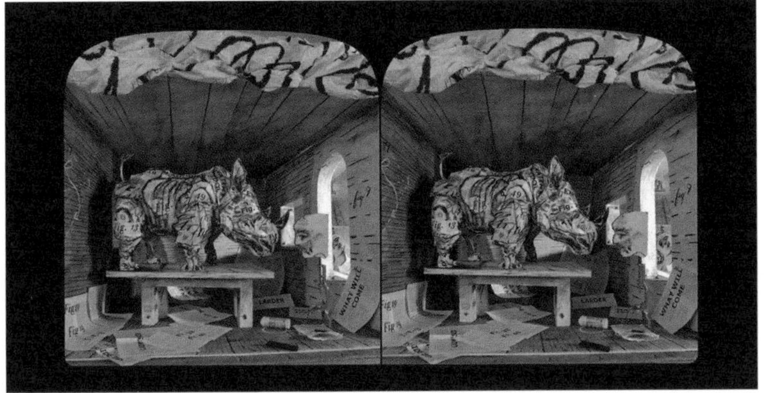

THE STEREOSCOPE: DRAWING WITH ONE EYE SHUT

In its most basic sense, a stereoscope brings our eyes in front of our head. In the centuries since Alberti and his treatise on vanishing point perspective, painting and image-making have been a monocular activity, turning a three-dimensional world into a two-dimensional surface, and then finding every way, from vanishing points to successivcly desaturating planes of color as elements in the picture plane ascend, assumed to be farther away, layers of hills getting paler and paler as they ascend the picture surface—to recreate the illusion of depth.

Stereoscopes, which developed almost at the same time as photography, are about the nature of binocularity. Biologically, humans are predators, with depth-perception but a narrow field of vision, as distinct from prey, with wide-angle vision to anticipate flight. To recapitulate from basics: we see everything twice. Right eye and left eye see two separate images, each of which obeys the Albertian rules of single-point perspective. Right eye, left eye. Right eye, left eye. Close one eye, and the image jumps. The two images are then combined in our brain to make an image of the world with depth that we move through and take for granted. Every moment we effortlessly combine the two images. This invisible double vision is what it is to see.

Two different photographs taken three inches apart, approximately the distance between my eyes. Two flat images. You can hold and touch the flatness. The sheet of card with two photographs. But looked at through the stereoscopic viewer, which converges and magnifies the image, we enter a strange world. The image is doubled: two photographs, two images overlapping. Slide the image closer or farther, and wait. There is a clear, discernible moment of transformation. The two become not just one, but a door to a different space. We are no longer looking at a photograph of a World War I battle scene. We are invited into the mud and debris.

Let us list the elements. The stereoscopic viewer has blocked off peripheral vision; our focus is kept on the photograph. We are looking through a magnifying glass; the image fills the whole range of vision. We look, not across the photograph, as we would look at a photograph of a battle scene, but into it, into its layers. Our eyes have to do the work. We have to activate the photo, converging and focusing at different focal distances to separate the different objects. But most important, what is natural becomes conscious. We realize that we are not seeing depth; we are constructing it. What is invisible becomes visible. The brain becomes a muscle, working to combine the two clearly different pictures into the single illusion. Our pleasure is again a pleasure at our self-deception—of the transformation of what we know to be two dimensions into the illusion of three dimensions, which we know to be false. This is something we, our own brains, have done. We are actively making the seeing. In the stereoscope, but of course in all our seeing, we are active participants, in the construction of depth in the image. The stereoscope becomes a machine for demonstrating seeing.

A RUNNING MAN: THE ZOETROPE

Zoetropes, praxinoscopes, phenakistoscopes. These machines were all precursors to moving photography: all are variations

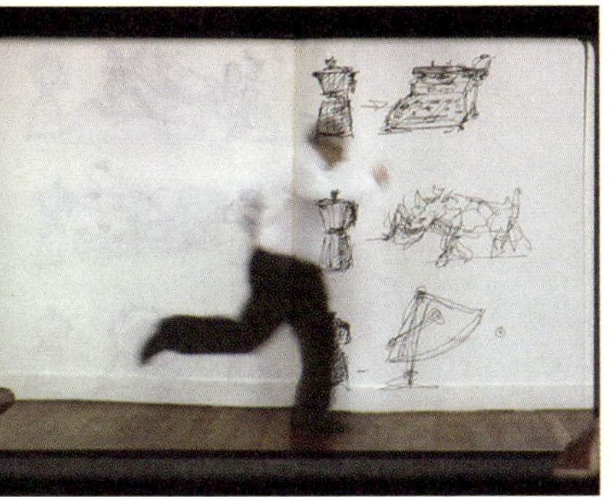

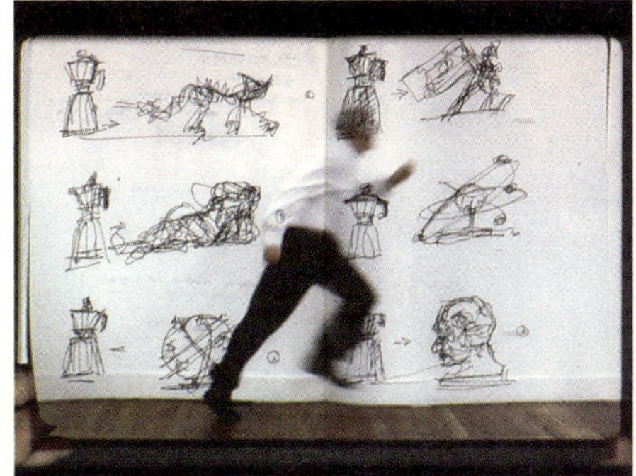

of machines for creating illusions of continuous movement. Through different techniques of revealing and then concealing images of an action in successive stages of completion—either using two rotating discs, or slits in a drum with images printed on the inside, or a faceted mirror—all these devices take a clearly still image and show us its transformation, not from flatness to depth, as in a stereoscope, but from stillness to motion.

I PHOTOGRAPH MYSELF WALKING

I step over a chair. I photograph the action twenty-four times at different stages. The foot leaving the floor. Leaning forward. Lifting the other foot. Missing the back of the chair. The new foot clearing the backrest. Stepping into the void. The front foot touching the floor. Project these images successively in front of the eye, and they are simply a blur. But have a way of freezing the image briefly, showing the next one, still again—using either the shutter and claw of a projector, or the slits of a zoetrope, which have the effect of a shutter—we have the figure in motion: the man climbs over the chair.

These machines are all circular, an action ending where it began so we can look at the spinning disc not just once, but see what appears as a continuous, cyclical movement. Someone rowing, playing leapfrog, skipping.

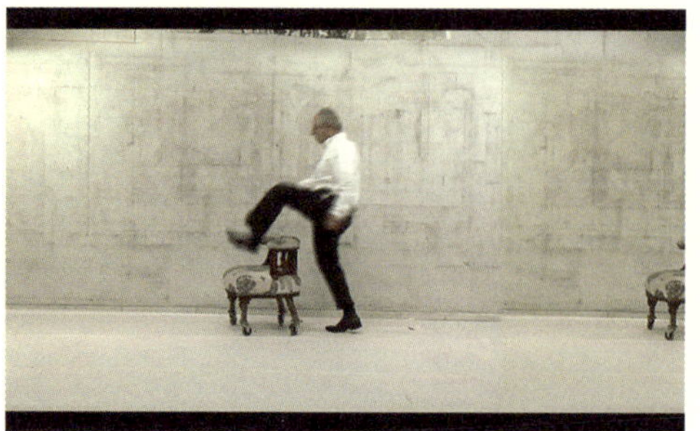

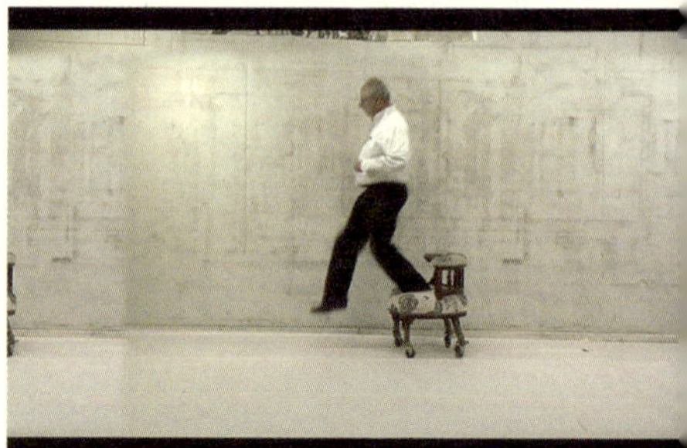

The man steps over the chair.
The man steps over the chair.
The man steps over the chair.
The man steps over the chair.

We have the double revelation. The primary one of the brain as muscle, again doing the work of turning stillness into movement, of making that which seems natural become the product of our own agency. And second, with the specifics of zoetropes, phenakistascopes, praxinoscopes, the specificity of the actual material, the object, the machine, the activity—which are stethoscopes for seeing, we observe our seeing through them. Listening to the whirring of a well-oiled brain.

They all involve rotation, coming back to where we began, only to repeat the action—the man climbing over the chair. No sooner is he done than another chair appears; he climbs over that one too. No sooner is he over that, than another one . . . We are both moving through time and stuck in it.

This is not the heart of a zoetrope, but it is what inevitably comes from it. The idea is produced by the material. At the edge of a narrative, hoping that this time, something new will happen: that he won't step over the chair, that he'll trip, that someone will meet him, that the chairs will come to an end—or THIS time. While at the same time, we know that nothing will change.

The pressure for the protagonist to escape his fate, to be able to escape the magnetic field of the zoetrope, to leave the circular orbit, to outrun his fate. We start with a visual, optical, biological effect, but we end with more. There is always more than the primary effect. And the invitation in the studio is to follow that "more"—what it is in the zoetrope, in the shadows, in the landscape, to follow other routes out of the cave.

Repetition is important. The zoetrope and escaping the zoetrope. The phrases on a list are repeated. A list of the points in a lecture as it is written.

THE HISTORY OF CINEMA #1
THE HISTORY OF CINEMA #2
PERFORMANCES OF TRANSFORMATION
DRAWING WITH ONE EYE SHUT
CHAPEAUISM
SYLLOGISM OF PRINTING
THE ILLUMINATING SHADOW
RUNNING BACKWARD
AS IF I COULD / DUK I FI SA

I find I repeat the list four or five times in different notebooks. Each time and repetition the phrases returning in the zoetrope. Each time I expect the list to be different; each time, to my surprise, it is the same, or almost the same. But in the re-ordering, the slight shift, the word that is illegible, we make some new crack, a new element enters the list, makes a space for itself—and this is the guest we have been waiting for.

REPEATING THE DRAWING

I make a drawing. It is done twice, thrice: a portrait. The repetition does not improve the likeness. Each time, there is an allowance for the arm to lead, to let the movement of the hand do the looking, as if the muscles of the hand, the wrist, the arm know what the face looks like. They don't. The drawings are torn into

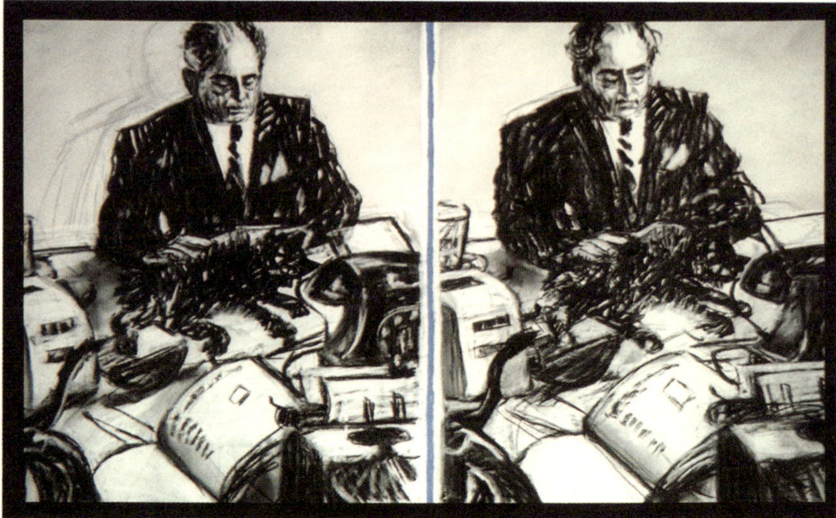

pieces. I tear down across the hairline, through the nose, separating the mouth, and then reconfigure them. The eyes, too far apart, are brought closer together. The moustache from drawing number 3 matches the nose from drawing number 4. The moving hand and the recognizing eye take over.

The work that the brain does, which we can feel in the coalescing of the two stereoscopic images into one image, has a similarity to the physical work in the studio—the moving of sticks, pieces of paper, mirrors, ink. This physical action is not only a provocation of the mental action but also a metaphoric description of it.

THE SYLLOGISM OF PRINTING: THE ETCHING PRESS

In the corner of the studio is a press for printing etchings. The press has a double metaphor.

On the one hand, intimate and domestic. There is the bed of the printing press, covered by blankets (thick felt) to protect

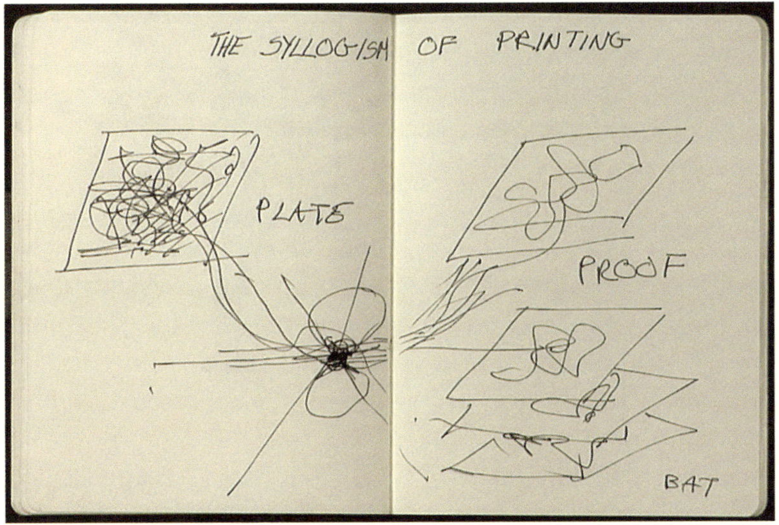

the sheet (the sheet of paper under the blanket). Under the blanket, on top of the sheet, we make sense of the open bite, the foul bite, the spit bite, the drypoint, the hard ground. An entire erotics of etching, a process that has an essential physical sensuousness: the gentle wiping of the hand, the soft ground, the open bite. The bubbles of the acid are feathered off, the soft ground is gently dabbed on, the ink is wiped off with the palm of the hand, the dampness of the sheet judged with the back of the hand.

But the etching press is also a primitive machine for logic. A plate is prepared: a proposition. Through acid, engraving burins, drypoint scratches, the pittings with the dot of an aquatint, the smooth surface of the plate is disturbed. It is inked, excess ink is cleaned off the surface, it goes through the bed of the press: the sheet of paper, the blanket. This layered collection—the blanket, the sheet of paper, the copper—passes under the rollers of the press, the paper pressed into the plate.

On the other side of the roller, the blanket and the sheet of paper are peeled back; and we have—a proof. The proof is a record of all the damage done to the plate. If the proof does not hold out, the proposition must be altered, the plate reworked, sent back through the rollers to reveal a new proof.

One thinks of the proof states of Rembrandt's *Three Crosses*. With each state, the proposition altered to produce a new proof. And so on, until the final proof is accepted, given the forensic stamp of approval: BAT *(bon à tirer)*.

The pressure at the center of the process, the meeting of the two rollers, one above the bed and one below the plate, in felt and paper and blankets—is an invisible moment, hidden by the blankets themselves. And this stands in for the moment of transformation. The artist as maker on one side, the artist as observer on the other side of the roller. And the best master-printer a mediator between the two. The transformation grows. It is also a transformation of the image, from copper to paper, and from one image to its mirror reversal.

Behind this I think of another layer, a separation of the print from the artist, or a secondary objectification. The drawing on the plate is external to the artist. The print itself has a different independence, strengthened by the fact, or at any rate the possibility, of multiplicity. The etching and other prints are essentially about multiplicity: the private impulse becomes a public opinion.

MIRROR AS MEMBRANE: THE CLAUDE GLASS

The Claude glass is another optical device for making us conscious of ourselves as viewers. It is named after the French landscape painter, as if using the glass could turn us all into Claude Lorrains. A well-polished copper etching plate becomes a mirror. Hold up the plate, and you see reflected in it a slice or a rectangle of the world behind you. Close one eye, and the image becomes a two-dimensional image on the surface of the plate. Adjust your position, or your arm, or the angle of the plate, and the rectangle of image is reframed. Hold your hand still.

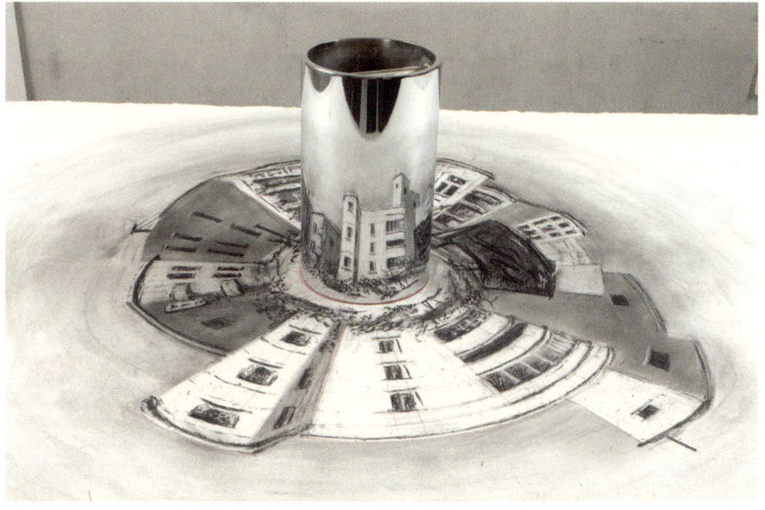

Hold the plate still, and you can transcribe the image with a drypoint needle directly onto the plate. The body becomes a crude mechanical camera, the copper the photographic plate. The stillness of the hand and the arm turn the body into a camera. The stillness of the arm and the plate are crucial elements. This is what reduces the infinity of projections coming toward us into a particular, limited, specific image.

SCREEN WITHOUT EDGE: ANAMORPHIC PROJECTION

On a table in the studio stands a cylindrical mirror. Under the cylindrical mirror, we place a circular piece of paper. The paper is reflected in the mirror. Draw a line on the paper; it is reflected (distorted) in the mirror. A straight line drawn becomes a parabola reflected on the mirror. To draw what appears to be a straight line in the mirror, we have to draw a particular curve on the paper. It is counter-intuitive drawing, not allowing the hand to make the familiar gestures and habits of a lifetime of how to make and achieve a particular shape within a drawing. To make an image we recognize as familiar in the mirror, an elongated distortion is needed.

Draw a rough line concentric to the edge of the paper: in the mirror we see a horizon line. The image in the mirror becomes a landscape. Brush some charcoal dust, and we have a cloud or dust in the foreground. This is straightforward. Let it be said, there is a great pleasure in re-learning how to draw, in constructing the distorted images in the service of the corrected image in the mirror.

But there are other transformations. Where does the landscape sit? Close an eye, and the landscape is on the surface of the mirror. Open both eyes, and the drawing floats and gathers different depths. Not an illusory depth of field, from faint distant mountains, or objects close to us being larger than distant objects; but a real depth. The image is somewhere behind the mirror. Not on a flat plane like the drawing, but occupying space. Different parts of the image are different focal distances from us; our eyes have to adjust to different focal distances.

From one position, the mirror presents itself as a rectangle. But we can circle the mirror, and the paper reflection, and the image does not come to an end. We are in a zoetrope. There are further secondary extensions and anomalies. We can see exactly 50 percent of the mirror, half a semi-circle of the cylinder; but the mirror can see 85 percent of the drawing. There is an apparent distortion in the mirror, and dislocation between the mirror and the drawing it reflects.

We are complicit in constructing the image, in transforming the distorted drawing on the paper into the illusion of recognizable coherence as received from the mirror. And in seeing, unavoidably, that our relation (here a physical one, but metaphorically too) to the image in the mirror is central to what it is.

And then we see the "more" that the mirror brings with it. The world as carousel, that which cannot be escaped; another kind of zoetrope, of circularity, turning around a center impossible to pin down. The image shifts backward and forward through what would be the center of the cylinder.

830 LAPS OF THE STUDIO

[WK walks around the stage.]

I walk around the studio, an endless circling of the space. Past the side of the table, go around the stepladder, circle the camera on its tripod, past the door to the balcony, past the table, turn around, reverse the journey. For ten minutes, for an hour. Gathering the floating fragments to start to draw or to start to write. Trying to get the fragments, the disconnected ideas and images to pull together—but in what way? Feeling the pressure for coherence—the relationship of the history of the camera to the activities in the studio, a zoetrope of thinking. While I know that the images or ideas will only clarify themselves in action—the charcoal on the paper, the ink in the book—I am unable to stop the walk. Sometimes stuck in the loop of a phrase that repeats itself:

TRUTH IS BEAUTY. BEAUTY, TRUTH.
TRUTH IS BEAUTY. BEAUTY, TRUTH.
THERE IS BEAUTY IN THE BELLOW OF THE BLAST.
THERE IS BEAUTY IN THE BELLOW OF THE BLAST.
TRUTH IS BEAUTY. BEAUTY, TRUTH.
O DEATH, WHERE IS THY STING?
O GRAVE, THY VICTORY?

WALKING & THINKING

Stuck in the zoetrope. The studio has become the zoetrope, and the repetitive action cannot be escaped. Knowing that the activity is both avoiding the questions to be found, and also essential. A productive procrastination. After 400 circuits, the man will finally escape his loop, will finally stop having to climb over the chair.

A walk without destination has a long history. From the ambulatories of the cloisters, a walk around a courtyard; to the promenades of aristocratic estates; to the *passiagata* of post-prandial conversation in nineteenth-century bourgeois cities. There is something in the action, of falling and catching yourself from falling in walking, the zoetrope-like repetition of the action: left foot, right foot, and go back to the beginning. Left foot, right foot, go back to the beginning. Something about the action that can provoke thinking—a change from the physical to the mental, a truce between the artist as maker and the artist as observer. The walk encompasses both elements. Images pinned to the wall, not looked at but visible, prods from the sideline. The books still sitting on the table. Yesterday's words on the page, not legible, but sending out waves of attraction and repulsion, reminding the artist of that which must be tackled. A walk which is the pre-history to a drawing.

MAKING A SAFE SPACE FOR STUPIDITY

[Text spoken over a montage of images, circling the stage.]

What is thought turned into action? Action sparking or provoking thoughts. How to put the different ideas, images, and fragments together, and parallel to that, a thinking in material.

[WK walks around the studio.]

There are two things going on here. To work with torn paper, the idea of sculpture; a magnetism of different materials and objects on the shelves around the studio. What physical material will propel the thought? Hoping to heat things up. To make a collision between a material and an idea.

There are in fact two figures walking in opposite directions. Trying to make sense of the idea of time and trying to find it in the material of the studio. Trying to find the transformation

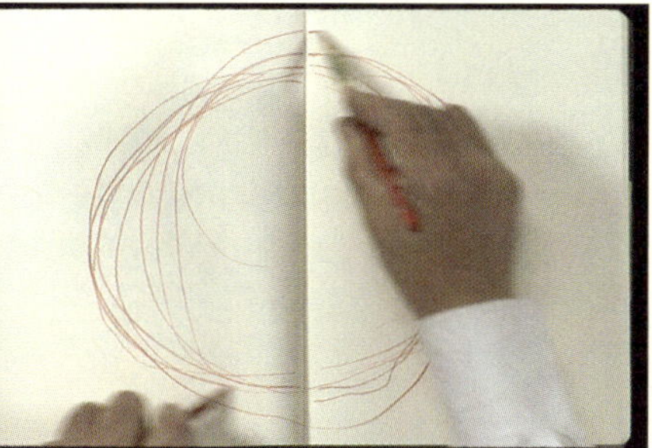

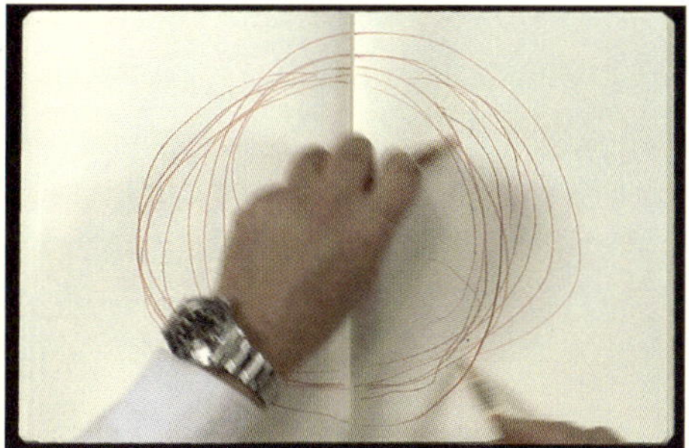

of different degrees of tension to squeeze an insight from the rock of stuck thought. Circling the ideas. The other self walks in the opposite direction, a hand reaching for the papers, scissors, rock, thinking about the walk itself. The studio as a brain. The 17m walk in the studio like the 4cm circle of synapses.

[WK 1 and WK 2 circle in opposite directions in the studio. Drawing hands speed up. Whirring egg beater.]

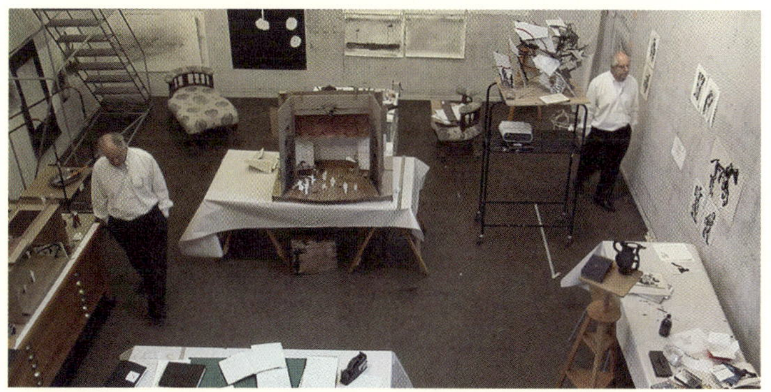

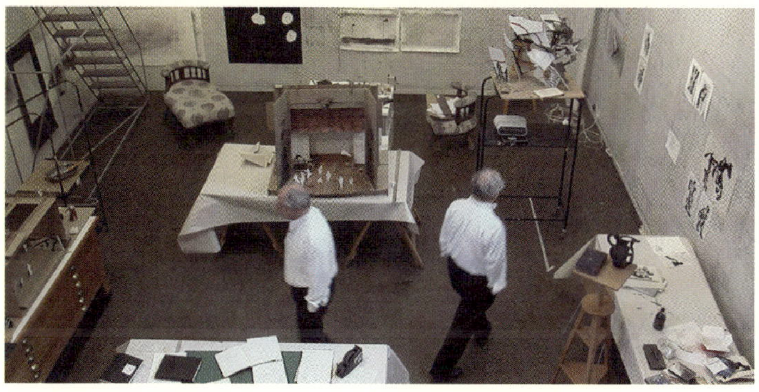

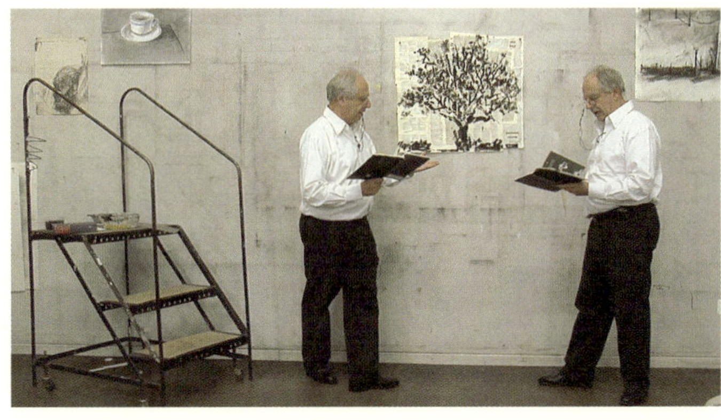

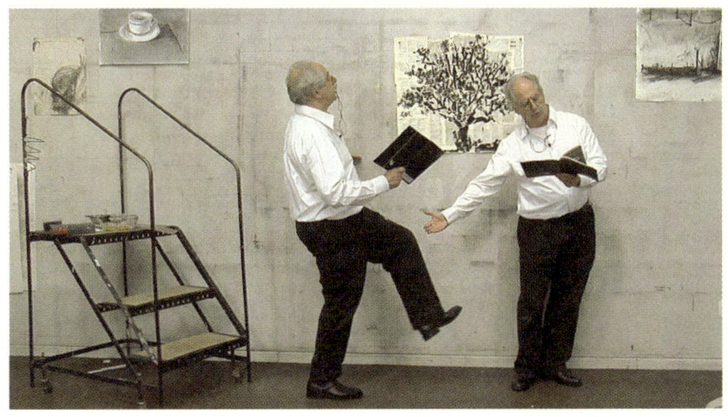

[WK perform extract of Lucky thinking from *Waiting for Godot.*]
[Cat & radio dance.]
[Paper house constructs itself.]

A collision, a particle collision, the double figure of the metaphor, the two figures circling, the orbits of the stars, the turn of the clock, the white chalk on paper, two pins needed to draw the eclipse of the orbit. A circus trainer in a top hat, whipping the horses moving around the studio, maybe two performing horses, circling.

[WK 1 and WK 2 speed up, circling the studio.]

To do this one needs to film in the studio. Twice two artists, four artists if I need two horses. But how to draw the collision?

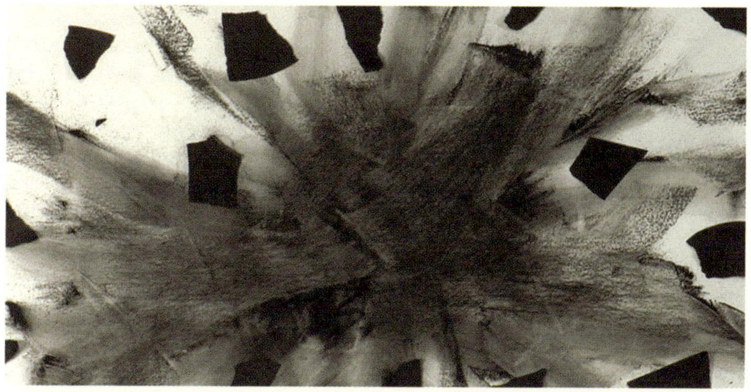

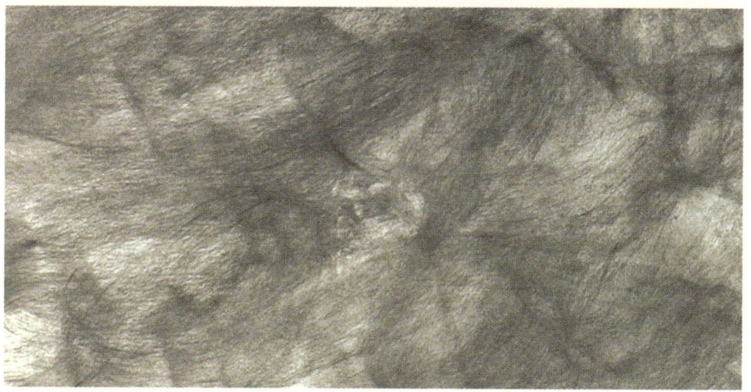

Alexander Calder's wire circus, with circuits speeding up, the orbits of the stars speeding up. The reciprocal movements of an egg beater. Taming the horse as a performer, or a double filming?

The camera in the studio becomes a place of holding, the walls of the studio an Eidophusikon, holding the time of the procrastinating walk. The walls of the studio, the inside of a cylindrical mirror, continuously circled. The metaphors can be extended until they get faster, and cannot hold.

[WK 1 and WK 2 collide and explode.]

The two circling men become Vladimir and Estragon.
"Nothing to be done."
"You know I am coming around to that view myself."

To locate where we are: we are in the studio, trying to parse the specific nature and activity of the studio, which can be characterized as making a safe space for stupidity.

This necessary stupidity is not the same as foolishness, or the innocence of the pure fool made wise through compassion. It is not the fool with license to talk truth to power. It is not a simple naïveté elevated. Rather it is making a space for uncertainty, for giving an impulse, an object, a material, the benefit of the doubt. Following the impulses that feel stupid, without a destination, believing that at some point, we will emerge from our zoetrope. It is more than this. It is a conscious repression of evaluating in advance of action the value of the thought. Allowing the work and the walk with its nonsense repeated mantras and words to take their time; to allow that which starts as a whim to continue.

To make a space for the inauthentic starting point. The foolish work of the six degrees of tension are there. A film is started without script or storyboard, a day is spent walking backward, throwing encyclopedias over your shoulder. Not in celebration of the stupidity itself, but believing in it more than in a studio of good ideas, of things worked out in advance and then shot and executed.

Understanding, hoping, believing, not out of conviction, but from physical experience, that from the physical making, from the very imperfections of technique—our bad backward walking—parts of the world, and parts of us, are revealed, that we neither expressed nor knew, until we saw them—when we realized we always did know them. Through the spaces opened by the stupidities themselves—the randomly torn pages, the line and the parabola—we enact, and see, and celebrate our construction of our world. This is how I make a horse. This is how I make a face. This is how I see. This is the space of the work in the studio.

END DRAWING LESSON FOUR

Drawing Lesson Five

IN PRAISE OF MISTRANSLATION

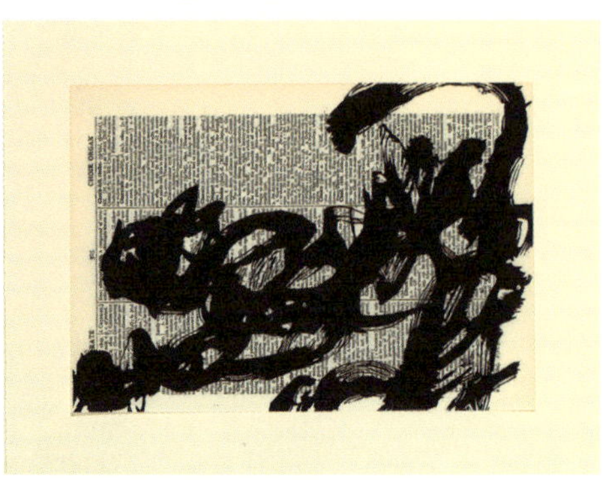

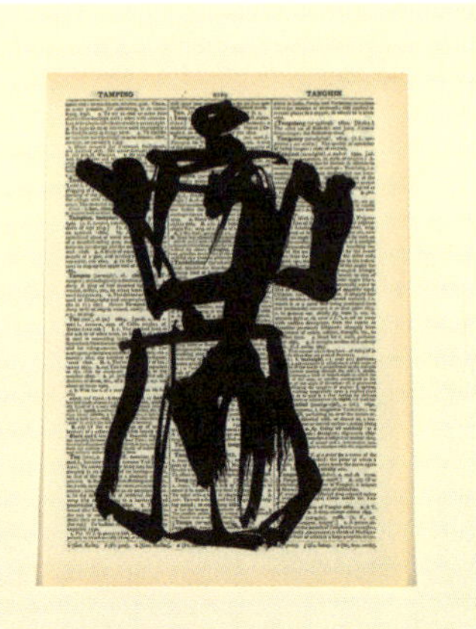

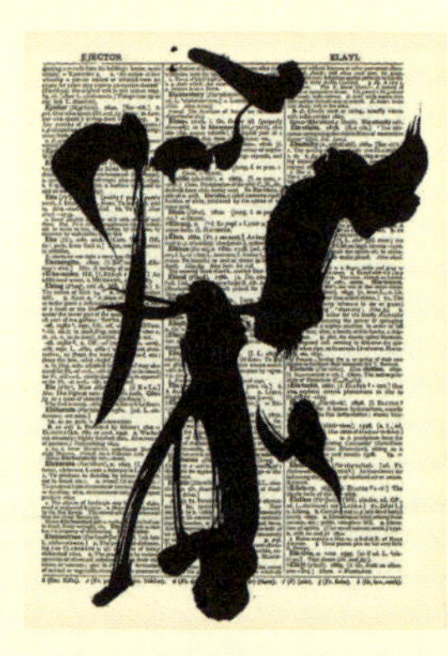

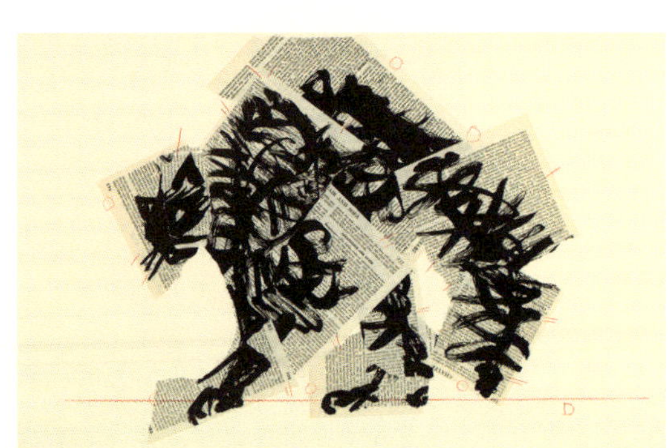

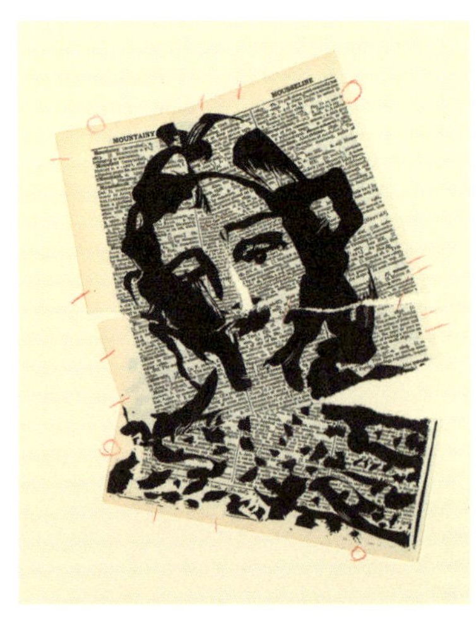

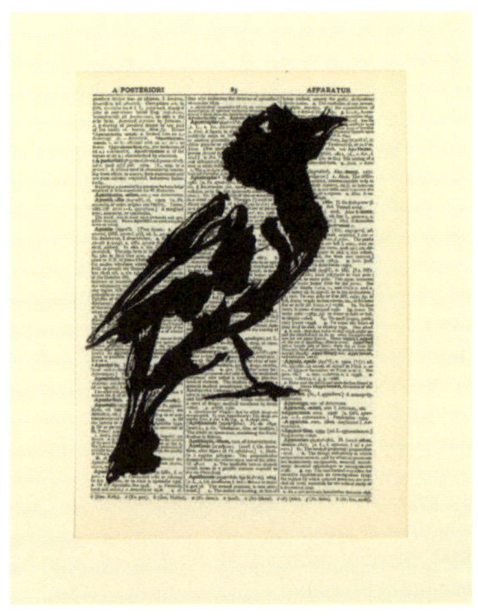

THIS fifth lecture has been the most difficult to write. It has taken longer than any of the others to launch. On the table, a fresh notebook. Sitting next to it, my pen filled with the best ink. Drawn up to the desk, my favorite chair—in which I could not sit. The words of the first sentence would not travel down my arm to my wrist and fingers.

I walked around the studio for two days. I started a series of linocuts to justify the delay in the writing.

[Show linocuts.]

A UNIVERSAL ARCHIVE (PARTS 4–17)

A coffee pot on my table. A further coffee pot. A fat inkwash drawing transferred to the lino and carved away to make . . . another coffee pot.

I looked at the list of thoughts I had written in preparation. Almost all of them I had used in lectures one to four. All the best ideas gone, crossed out, leaving me only with scraps.

The question that started the lecture at the beginning—ANYTHING TO SAY—reared up. I made a linocut of the text. YOU BROUGHT THIS ON YOURSELF! was the line I kept repeating. I made a linocut of the phrase.

I had new Chinese brushes, India ink, an encyclopedia to disembowel; the notes of the lecture could be left on the table. I continued with the drawings for the linocuts. A cat. A typewriter. Peonies in a vase. A rhinoceros. A linocut with a splash of ink, and the blank page in the center.

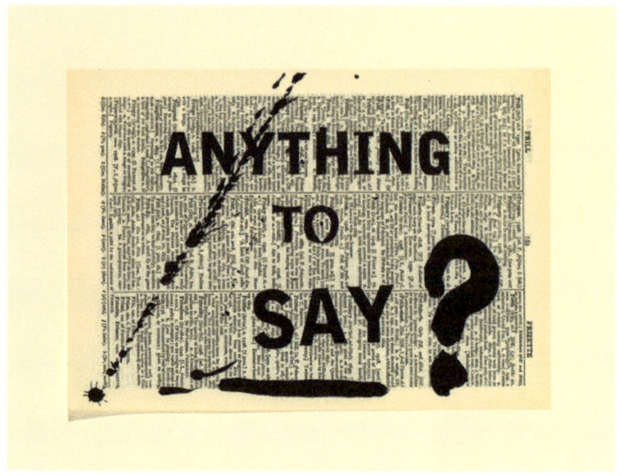

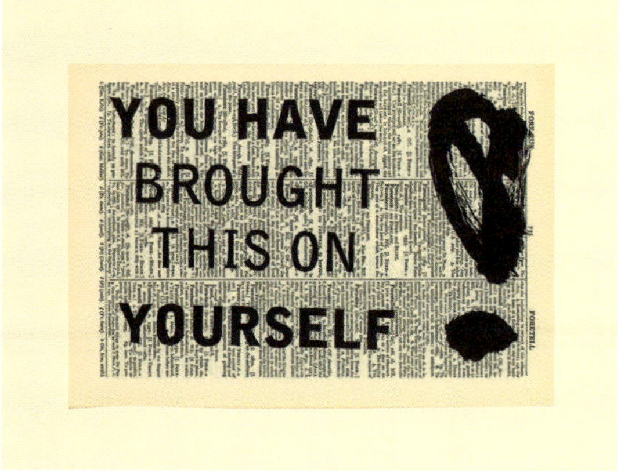

What was left in the notes? A corner of a superannuated bestiary. The notes read:

Dürer's rhinoceros
Rilke's panther
A note on cats and dogs
A bull
Picasso's goat
A return to horses
The asen

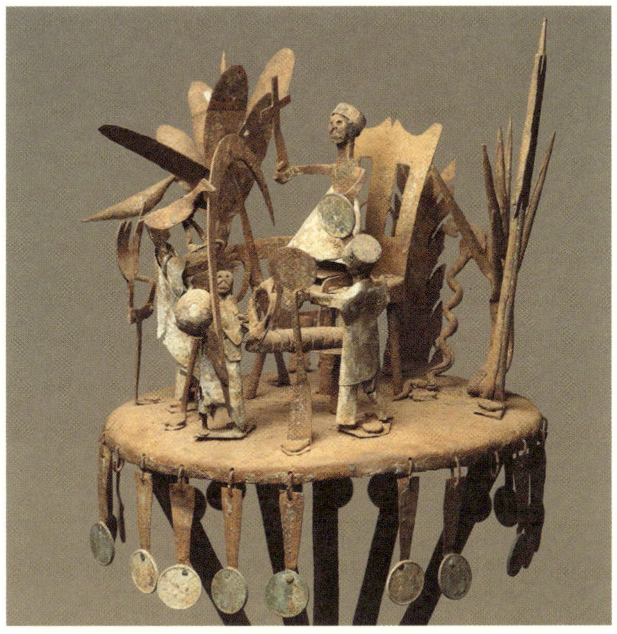

Between writing the list and writing the lecture, several months had passed.

What is an asen? An asen is an iron disk on a pole. Cut-out sheet metal of figures and objects. A disk about a foot in diameter.

We have a miniature stage filled with actors and scenery, isolated from the world by the pole on which it stands. A flag; a tree; a man with a ball; a girl on a chair.

A similarity to some paintings of Paul Klee and Jean Arp, in which a leaf can stand for a tree, and in which the radical change of scale implies a system of representation and narrative closer to the logic of dreams and their associations than the rationality of waking hours. The flag is higher than the banana tree. The chair is the size of the flag. Have the chair and its girl grown? Has the tree, which is now just a leaf, shrunk? Is the man next to the chair holding a ball, or the moon? Perhaps both. We look at a tableau, a frozen moment from a performance, a fixed charade, in which each object has a specific meaning, a hierarchy of figures and objects to convey a specific concept or sentence. A rebus, waiting to be read.

I read that an asen is a monument to a dead person. Originally from Benin, on the west coast of Africa, asen were made initially only for kings and the aristocracy, as objects through which one could invoke the spirit of the dead person. During the last century, they became common, as craftsmen who made curio objects for the tourist trade now made up altar-pieces to the specification of anyone who could afford one.

There are three people involved in the making of an asen. A dead person to be honored; the commissioner or donor of the piece, who briefs the maker; and the maker, or craftsman, himself. The choice of objects and figures on the asen comes from associations the donor makes to the dead person: his occupation, objects prized; but also from words, from the sounds of words of objects, rather than their literal representation. Between the briefing by the donor and the making of the asen, there is a gap. A list of requests from the donor, and a configuration of solutions and responses to these from the craftsman.

The asen becomes a rebus, a text made up of the words embedded in the images, a private riddle to be read. But then time passes, the donor joins the subject of the asen in death; he is not alive to remember his questions, to link the craftsman to the answers. The riddle remains in the museum. We lose the traces of the specific trio that contributed to the piece. The dead man, the donor, the craftsman. But the piece does not become mute. We are left with the leaf that is a tree, the flag, the girl on a chair, the ball that is a moon. There is an invitation to make our own rebus from the elements, a narrative sentence from the different pieces.

We can draw a lock. A bee. The number 4. A sheep. Some lips. And we can make the sentence:

LOCK B4 SHEEP LIP.
LOCK BEFORE EWE LIP.
LOOK BEFORE YOU LEAP.

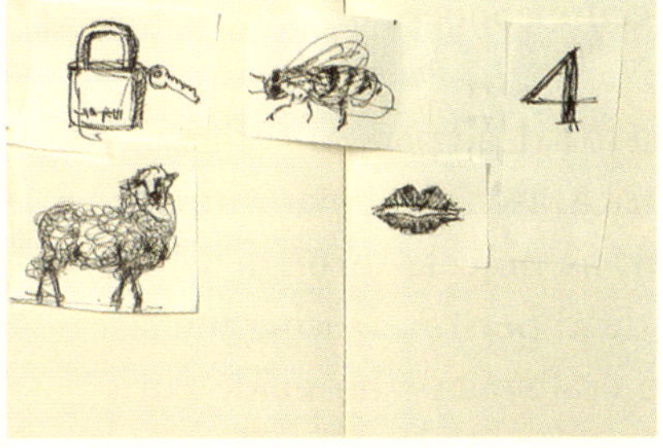

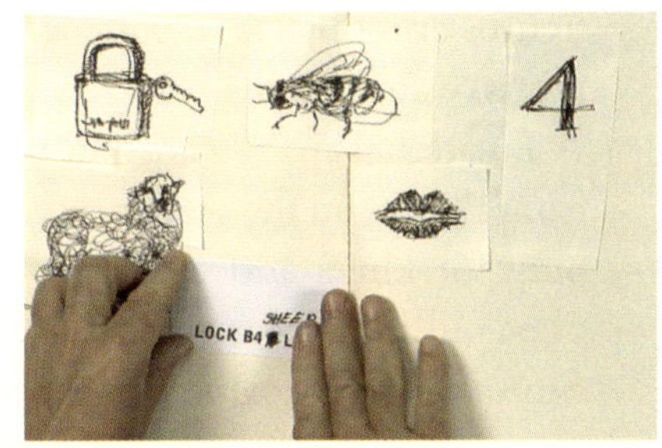

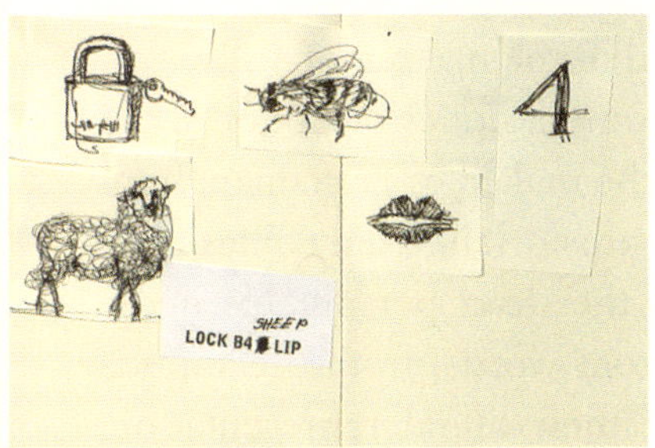

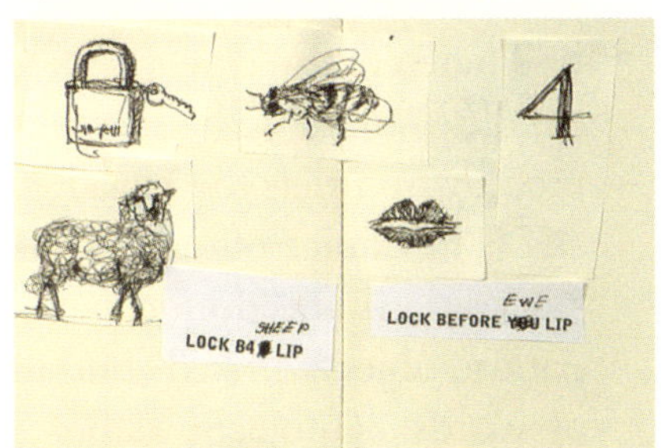

Or we can read it as:
KEEP YOUR LIPS SEALED TO AVOID BEING STUNG.

This rebus is just an extension of the children's autograph book message:

Y Y U R
Y Y U B
I C U R
Y Y 4 ME

Too wise you are
Too wise you be
I see you are
Too wise for me

Or:

FUNEX
SVFX
FUNEM
SVFM
OKMNX

Have you any eggs?
Yes, we have eggs.
Have you any ham?
Yes, we have ham.
OK, ham and eggs.

(This last one from my grandfather, who gave me the book of great landscapes I referred to in lecture two.)

And alongside it are the meaning's leavings, the coded letters in the graphic form, the graphic form of the tree, the chair, the flag; a West African rock, paper, scissors. Flag covers chair. Chair devours tree. Tree entangles flag.

The invitation is to make our own asen, our own translation of the objects into a sentence. To make the story—if not literally, then to feel the possibility of extrapolation from the object.

To make our own asen—folded paper and cardboard, cutout figures—take the rhinoceros, the different linocuts, put them together, make a miniature theater in which the objects can be slid about, repositioned, to make a sentence on the stage. Changing subject and object. Different stories provoked by different configurations of the drawings.

Again it does not have to be realized, but we are left with the possibility of making such a construction. I walk around the studio feeling the air, feeling the form of a possible asen. Dürer's rhinoceros, Rilke's panther, a tree made from a leaf, the flag, folded cardboard, folded steel. It is felt, physically, in the pectoral muscles, in the wanting of the arm to take the materials. An asen of a head and a jug or a chair.

A walk around the studio as possibilities multiply. NOT knowing the answer to the riddle opens all the possibilities and different possible answers. A riddle with a clear answer stops us short. The riddle of the sphinx—

> "What walks on four legs in the morning,
> Two legs at noon,
> Three legs in the evening?"

—is answered and leaves no trace.

We see the infant, the adult, the old woman. What is left of the riddle is a residue, the evocation of a life condensed into a day. This is one riddle that is not answered. Or the ongoing unfathomability of a sphinx itself, the double creature, the shift between what is human and what is not. The riddle with the answer leaves behind the secondary riddle, of that which does not have an answer.

THE OVERDETERMINED IMAGE

While we think of fantastical creatures, let us consider Dürer's rhinoceros, made in 1515. As I have understood, a rhinoceros was sent to the King of Portugal, and from him to Pope Leo X. While on the journey from Portugal to Italy, the ship carrying the rhinoceros was lost in a storm. The ship and the rhinoceros in its cage in the hold sank to the bottom of the sea off the coast of Italy. As a forensic record of the gift, Dürer was asked to make an image of the drowned animal. Having no model in front of him, he was reduced to making an identikit image based on reports from others who had seen the rhinoceros, or who had spoken to someone who had reportedly seen the creature.

Somewhere behind the image, there was an animal. But the image is overloaded with all the projection of Dürer's interlocutors, of Dürer's conjectures, and of the history of woodblock chapbooks of imagined creatures, griffins, sphinxes. Dürer makes a woodcut rather than an engraving. The crude medium both conveying gaps in knowledge and trying to convince,

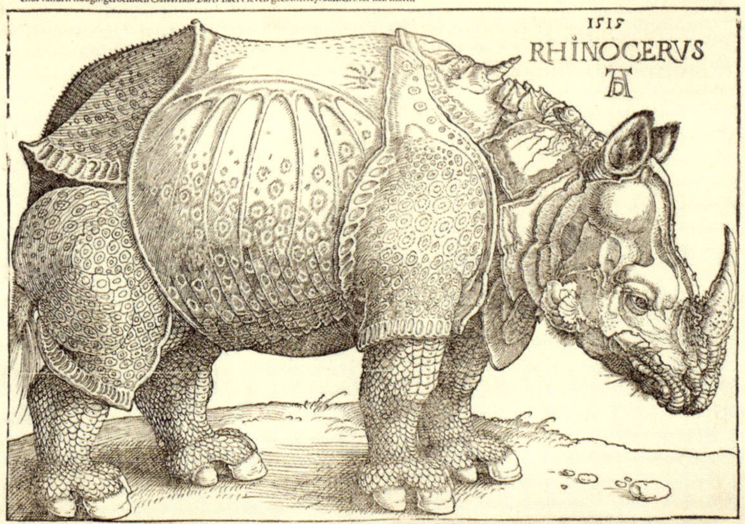

rather than to describe or report. The animal oscillates between being of this world, an animal observed, and coming from a completely other universe, being made more and more impossible. Being familiar, and becoming other.

The rhinoceros in the woodcut is covered with armored plating, what appear to be rivets holding the plates of armor together. There is a secondary horn on the shoulder, like the small horn on the breastplate of a horseman in a full suit of armor at a tournament. A scalloped plate on its hindquarters is both of fabric and a metal skirt. But the eye looks forward, at odds with the hard carapace with which the body is covered. The eye of the rhinoceros is the punctum of the image, of the other, that which we are not. The ambiguity toward nature—wanting to pull it closer while wanting to proclaim its otherness. This is not just in Dürer.

In Pietro Longhi's painting of a rhinoceros of 1751, we see the rhinoceros at the carnival in Venice. The domestication of the rhinoceros becomes clearer. This was Clara, a celebrated rhinoceros that was taken on a tour of Europe by its impresario owner, a Leiden-based sea captain, between 1741 and 1751. Five men, two women, and a child observe the rhinoceros. Its horn has been cut off. One of the men holds it in his hand. And there is a rebus here: rhinoceros, horn, masks on one of the women and four of the men. An eighteenth-century Venetian asen. And we try to answer the rebus of this asen for ourselves.

Solution 1: Castration

The horn is an obvious phallus. And still today, more than ever, rhinoceri face extinction because of this metaphor. The horn looks like a phallus, and so is taken for one. The compressed hair of it is ground down to make an aphrodisiac. This is not a question of art history scholarship. This is about gangs armed with GPS devices that track the microchips in the rhino's horn; AK 47 assault rifles to shoot the rhinoceros and dissuade any game wardens from trying to disrupt the industry; and Interpol trying to intercept containers of rhino horns. Trials of veterinarians and game wardens complicit in the trade continue in Johannesburg today. The ambiguities in Longhi's painting are still with us.

To go back to the rebus of an asen: the power of the rhinoceros is transferred to the man with the horn, its potency. He is cuckolding a man in the center of the group. Let it be said that I am not good at solving riddles—I am not convinced by this reading at all. The black cloaks and the angled black hats of the men repeat the dark angularity of the animal. A Rorschach blot across the fold of the railing of the wooden fence that divides the painting in two.

Solution 2

A Great Chain of Being—another reading. Women at the top of the pyramid, distinguished also by the colors of their clothes; then the men, already halfway to rhino in the dark cloaks and their desaturated colors; and right at the bottom, not quite the rocks and stones of a medieval chain of being, but straw, and what appears to be a stone, but what I suspect is a pile of rhino feces.

Solution 3

Another reading of the rebus: "14th of February, 1751. This is what happened today. A rhinoceros near Piazza San Stefano. Attended with family. Then to supper."
Simply a record of what was seen.

The painting most probably encompasses all of these. But as with Dürer's rhinoceros, the animal is both pulled toward us and pushed away. It is given a name, Clara, as though it is a family member, brought into the theater but then marveled at for its very difference and distance. We want it to be like us—come and eat from my hand—but we need the barrier to keep it away, not just for fear it will trample us, but to reassure ourselves of its difference, its place on another rung of the Chain of Being.

This domestication of nature continues. Not only in the killing of rhinoceri for their horns—they are farmed like cattle, but not yet for their horns, still for their exotic otherness. There are contradictory reversals in Johannesburg society. Game reserves with their so-called wildlife are the safest places to be. Holiday resorts, where we have recreational danger. I could illicitly leave the Range Rover and taunt the elephant, but I don't; and at night in the rest camp, there is sleep, untroubled by any night dangers. It is in the city that the real wildlife exists, where one has to look over one's shoulder at every stop sign. People who used to keep rhinoceri on their manicured lawns have ceased to, not from fear of the animals themselves, but from fear of the men with the guns, coming not to burgle the houses but to shoot the rhinoceri and carry off their horns.

And let us not deny their extraordinary otherness. We are looking at something that feels closer to a stegosaurus, something that takes us far back in time.

We are captivated by the animals, and I count myself as one of those held. There is something in the weight of the huge head, in the barrel broadness of the body, in the dexterity and delicacy of movement, the crossing of a front foot as it trots. There is a mixture of what the rhinoceros brings and what we project onto it. The lightness of its gait, as if it could be a dancer; its connection to a deeply ancient past, more dinosaur than contemporary mammal; and of course every rhinoceros brings with it Dürer, Longhi, Ionesco, its very plates of armor weighed down by the history of expectation of what a rhinoceros is, or can become. The mass of it: bone, muscle, grit—how can it fill its own volume? All its effort and strength going into becoming itself. That embodiment tucked into a sketchpad.

There is something inside us that reaches toward the otherness of the animal—as if the animal itself can lead us to the unfathomable otherness that resides inside us—a part of us that we cannot reach but that we can see in the very non-humanness of the animal. We anthropomorphize the animal, not to say it is like us, but to get closer to that part of it and us that we cannot reach.

HAVING A GOOD SEAT

What is a horse?

Girl no. 20, define a horse.

Girl no. 20 thrown into greatest alarm by this request.

(This is Charles Dickens in Chapter Two of *Hard Times*. The interrogator is the school owner, the Platonic Mr. Gradgrind.)

Girl no. 20 unable to define a horse.

Blitzer, define a horse.

Quadruped. Graminivorous. Forty teeth, namely, twenty-four grinders, four eye teeth, and twelve incisors. Sheds coat in spring in marshy countries. Sheds hoofs too. Hoofs hard, but requiring to be shod in iron. Age known by marks in mouth. This and more, Blitzer.

Now, Girl no. 20, said Mr. Gradgrind, you know what a horse is.

Quadruped—tail and mane—that is enough to draw a horse.

But a horse is also exactly the right scale for the magnification of a man: for making him magnificent. A man standing on a chair or a table is ridiculous. On a pedestal, we begin to let him grow. But put the man on a horse, and preferably the horse on a pedestal, and you have a hero or a tyrant, or at any rate, someone who has made a name for himself. A horse fits so snugly under the legs. It feels not just connected to the person, but part of him, an extension of the person to show who he really is. We make the horse part of us, an attribute or demonstration of our own might; the horse becomes an anthropomorphic prop.

But more than that, we absorb the horseness into ourselves, an uprightness of posture, from Marcus Aurelius on the Campidoglio in Rome, to Verrocchio's mercenary in Venice, Bartolomeo Colleoni. Here the power of the horse is transferred one more layer. The eye of the horse, and the eye of the Commendatore. To Simon Bolivar at the entrance of Central Park, being a man is not enough, even a rhinoceros horn is not enough. For Marshal Zhukov, on his horse outside the Kremlin in Moscow, even sitting on a horse is not enough; he stands in the stirrups, a child on tiptoe playing at riding. The ghost of Don Quixote and Rocinante follows them all. We suck in the energy and strength of the animal, then sit up straight, to show we are worthy of the transfer of power. Through our posture, convincing the horse of our divine right to ride him.

In Italo Svevo's *Confessions of Zeno*, Zeno, recently married, reflects on his new state: "He realised he was so contented in his new role, that he found himself assuming the pose of the different equestrian statues they had seen in the squares of the towns they had visited on their honeymoon." The houyhnhnm-like moral good of the horse is transferred through a demand for posture (the horse as teacher of deportment) to the man, even when the horse, the founding principle of the action, has gone.

Like Cockney rhyming slang, in which the explanatory term disappears, leaving only the verbal effect. Your feet, in Cockney rhyming slang, are your "plates of meat," "feet" and "meat" rhyming. But then we don't say "plates of meat," we only say "plates," as in, "I must get off my plates," or "My plates are killing me." If the asen-maker is gone, we don't know the meat, only the uncomfortableness of standing on plates, to be walked on with care. The horse has been consigned to the knacker's yard, but we keep the posture.

In the studio, this need and not need, this reduction and extrapolation, is there in the physical transformation. The horse becomes a series of jointed paper pieces, or four sticks and a door handle, to bring the heroics of a horse down to tabletop size, to take away its authority. This is not possible. A broomstick and a stuffed sock, and on top of this hobbyhorse, any child is Marcus Aurelius.

CONCERNING CATS AND DOGS

A cat is a line, a dog is a dot. The principle of a cat is its spine. Draw any line, add some fur, some ears and whiskers, and you have a cat. A dog is its nose. Its movement, its being led by its nose. A point leading the way. An arrow, at best a vector, across a page. In working with puppets, you can take a feather boa, put a tennis ball at one end, two sticks to support and manipulate the boa, and you have a cat that can sidle, rub itself against your legs, turn in on itself. Shake one hand, and the cat's hips twitch before making a leap. For a dog you need a head, to indicate the direction of the nose, and a tail, to comment on the nose's findings.

We can pull our cat and dog further. We do not need to make puppets of them. But let them inform the performance of an actor. A performance incorporating catness into the body, the voice, the movement, of an actor, becomes a performance of indifference. Fill the actor with a dog, and however hard he tries, there is a residual stupidity. A whole reading of Godot could be done with this cat and this dog.

> Cat: Nothing to be done.
> Dog: I'm beginning to come around to that opinion. All my life I've tried to put it from me, saying, Vladimir, be reasonable. You haven't tried everything yet. And I resumed the struggle.

Or, Antonio from *The Merchant of Venice:*

> In sooth, I know not why I am so sad. It wearies me.
> The cat: ??

Or in *The Seagull*—

> Medvedev, dog: Why do you always wear black?
> Masha, cat: I am mourning, for my life.

There is a circling of the lines, as they twist, of the cat, gently turning.

Or we could do it the other way around, Estragon as dog, Vladimir as cat. Both work. In any event, it is taking some attribute outside us, its catness, its dogness—something we can observe, something we can become expert in, absorbing it. It is outside of us, but it corresponds to something in us, which we hope it will attach to, and grow and make clearer. But there is also reverse transmogrification.

DOMESTICATING THE BICYCLE

The Irish writer Flann O'Brien, in his book *The Third Policeman,* talks of metamorphosis, but not of animals: "The gross and net result of it, is that people who spent most of their natural lives riding on bicycles over the rocky roadsteads of this parish, get their personalities mixed up with the personalities of their bicycles. As a result of interchanging of the atoms of each of them. And you would be surprised at the number of people in these parts who are nearly half people and half bicycles. . . When a man lets things go so far that he is more than half a bicycle, you will not see him as much, because he spends a lot of his time leaning with one elbow on walls, or standing propped up by one foot on kerbstones."

PICASSO'S BICYCLE

The transmutation of atoms

This transmutation of atoms we see in another bicycle. Picasso's bull. Bicycle seat and bicycle handlebar switch atoms—in both directions. The bicycle becomes a bull. The dessicated skull and horns of a dead bull, ears gone, hide turned to the leather of the saddle; but the bull also retreats into a bicycle. We make the other familiar. The duende of the bull reduced to a Raleigh 28″ bicycle, in order to reinvigorate the quotidian. The lees, the residue of the metaphor, the skeleton of the bicycle, filled with new possibilities.

PICASSO'S WICKER BASKET

Another domestic scrapyard. Picasso's goat. Here we have not one transformation but a series of them that together constitute the goat. A life made of scrap, found objects; all can be consumed. The basket becomes ribs. The plumbing pipe, an anus. Ceramic jugs for udders. A palm frond for the slope of the goat's back. A small palm frond for the snout. Held together with plaster. Turned into an absence, its mold; transformed into wax; and then turned into bronze.

But what holds us here is not just recognition—the bicycle bars like horns, the saddle like a skull (the making of a bull: I put a bicycle in a hat, and pull out a bull)—but with the goat, we have a gathering of potential. A meeting between a strengthening image of a nanny goat, and the elements found in the scrapyard next to Picasso's studio at Valloris. We see the chaos combining. The work of transformation. We are learning the grammar of the goat.

We see it through all that is NOT transformed. The plaster that holds the elements together and completes the sculpture. The sculpture is a demonstration of the action of making the world. We have the goat, the sum of everything it has consumed, palm fronds, straw basket; this omnivore now repeated, demonstrated, in the making of the goat. All is possible. Picasso is making the goat. He is thinking of height, width of shoulders, shape of hoof, size of palm frond to hips, width—he is deep in the making. But of course, we see more. We see the goat, to be sure. But also a sense of the world that can be constructed—an ad hoc assembly of fragments that reach toward us, taking these fragments and making our own asen.

We run the film in reverse. We see the goat. We see the constituent parts sitting in the studio. We see them dispersed among the debris of the scrapyard, Picasso carefully placing each in the camouflage of the other ceramic fragments, garden refuse, of abandoned bicycles. We run it forward quickly, and we see the whirlwind that gathers the pieces, that makes from such chaos this beast—a beast not slouching toward Bethlehem, to be born again, but standing four-square in front of us, ready for anything that lies ahead.

Transformation, metamorphosis is of course the bread and butter of animation. Something difficult to do on the stage, a cat turning into a telephone. But invited to happen, with charcoal and eraser. A disintegration, a space opened up . . . A potential . . . A landing of something else.

[Show paper confetti.]

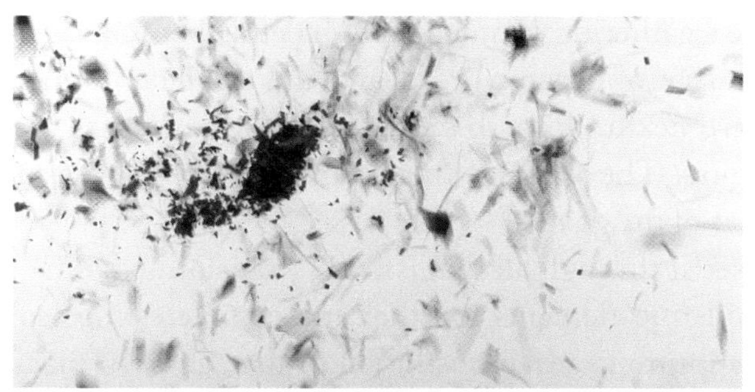

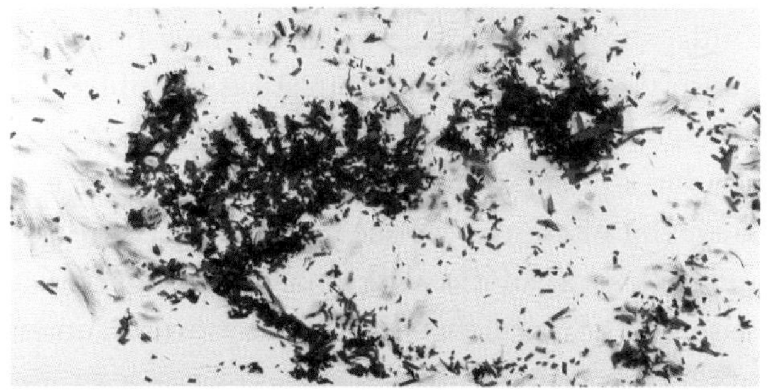

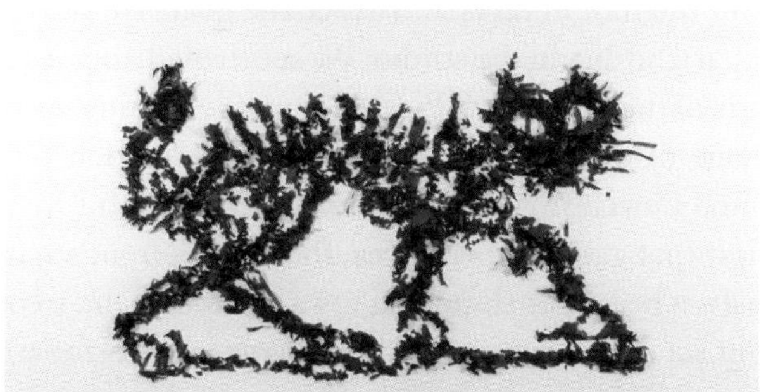

MONTAGE OF CAT TRANSFORMATIONS

1. Cat emerges from a radio *(Ubu Tells the Truth)*
2. A blind embosser becomes a cat *(Stereoscope)*
3. A cat becomes a bomb *(Stereoscope)*
4. An explosion of burnt paper shards becomes a cat *(Anti-Mercator)*
5. Espresso pot becomes a cat *(Lexicon)*

6. Cat becomes a telephone *(Sobriety, Obesity & Growing Old)*
7. A coffee pot becomes a cat *(Sobriety, Obesity & Growing Old)*
8. The cat becomes a gas mask *(Sobriety, Obesity & Growing Old)*
9. Cat becomes a megaphone *(Sobriety, Obesity & Growing Old)*

PRODUCTIVE MISTRANSLATION

When she was about three years old, I told my daughter Alice a story. Once upon a time, a dog and a cat were in the garden. The cat was teasing the dog. The dog chased the cat. The cat ran through the cat-flap into the kitchen and escaped the dog. Later that day, Anne, my wife, asked Alice what story I had told her. She repeated the story. A cat and a dog were in the garden. The dog chased the cat. The cat flapped his wings and escaped.

Here it is all offered. The concept of a cat-flap in the door was not comprehended, and so it was replaced with the flap of familiar wings. The story is understood: the cat and the dog in the garden, the chase, then there was a garbled section, a piece of text missing, and the escape. And a pressure not to accept the broken bridge, the word not understood; a narrative need—more than a narrative need, a demand for comprehension, a demand to put the fragments together into a whole, to turn the cat into a griffin, to reach its escape. To respond to a crisis with an imaginative transformation. For the cat, the crisis of being chased by the dog; for Alice, the crisis of not understanding a word.

This is Ovid. Tereus's wife and her sister are fleeing from Tereus. He chases them through the rooms of the palace. They are in a panic of escape. This is Ovid in the voice of Ted Hughes:

> As he saw the sisters running,
> now his bellow was homicidal, as it was anguished.
> He came after them,
> and they who had been running seemed to be flying.
> And suddenly they were flying.

One swerved
on a wing into the forest.
The other, with blood still on her breast,
Flew up under the eaves of the palace.
And Tereus,
Charging blind,
In his delirium of grief and vengeance,
No longer caring what happened,
He too was suddenly flying,
On his head and shoulders a crest of feathers,
Instead of his sword, a long, curved beak.

He had become a wood hoopoe. Alice did not specify the species of bird the cat had become—it was generic griffin.

A later example. I was speaking on the telephone to a friend, Basil, and I asked him what his husband, Adrian, was busy with. "Oh," he said. "Adrian is making a tree search." A tree search? Of course, a tree search is an Internet term. You search for a word, a trunk, and from this flow many branches which you can follow, to smaller and smaller twigs, refining the search, until you find the information on your particular branch. Or leaving that branch, returning to the trunk and following another branch. You can zoom out and see the branch you are on in relation to all the other facets of information, all the other parts of the tree: a tree search. At the end of the conversation, I asked Basil what Adrian was researching.

"What do you mean?"

"You said he was doing a tree search."

"No," he said. "I said he was making a T-shirt."

A tree search is less interesting than a griffin, but let's follow it. For the first instant, I was stopped by not knowing what it was. I felt stupid. But almost at the same time, I saw and constructed the principles of a tree search. Even as I grew the tree inside me, it was as if it had always been there. I could envisage it on the computer screen, the drawing of the tree, the blocks of text on the branches—and cursed myself for not remembering immediately what it was. On the one hand, it is a superego caring for us, protecting us from revealing our ignorance, performing as if we knew what we were talking about.

But it is more than that, even if only as a by-product, as a result of the self-protective thinking. This need for making sense of the world using all means possible, of using whatever pieces we can find in the scrap heap—a computer screen, a photo of a tree, a diagram of a flow-chart, fragments of text—to complete the sense of the world.

A route map again. We have come from Plato to the colonies, specifically Africa, to the city of Johannesburg, to the studio in the city (in the last lecture); and now we are in the bookshelf in the studio, with Ovid, Flann O'Brien, and Rilke—looking at images and words, looking at the productivity of mistranslation.

Der Panther
Im Jardin des Plantes, Paris

Sein Blick ist vom Vorübergehn der Stäbe
so müd geworden, daß er nichts mehr hält.
Ihm ist, als ob es tausend Stäbe gäbe
und hinter tausend Stäben keine Welt.

Der weiche Gang geschmeidig starker Schritte,
der sich im allerkleinsten Kreise dreht,
ist wie ein Tanz von Kraft um eine Mitte,
in der betäubt ein großer Wille steht.

Nur manchmal schiebt der Vorhang der Pupille
sich lautlos auf—. Dann geht ein Bild hinein,
geht durch der Glieder angespannte Stille—
und hört im Herzen auf zu sein.

Rainer Maria Rilke, 6.11.1902, Paris

The Panther at the Jardin des Plantes
Rainer Maria Rilke, Paris 1902

Ceaselessly the bars and rails keep passing
Til his gaze, from weariness, lets all things go, for
it seems to him the world consists of bars and
railings, and beyond them the world exists no more.

Supple, strong, elastic is his pacing
and its circle much too narrow for a leap
like a dance of strength around a centre
where a mighty will was put to sleep.

Yet from time to time, the pupils' curtain
rises silently. An image enters, flies through
the limbs' intensive stillness
until, entering the very heart, it dies.

(translation by Richard Exner)

The poem is in German, which I do not have. I only know the poem in translation; and so, of course, the poem multiplies. There is no correct translation—only a series of circlings of the poem, of what it might be in English. Every translation is a mistranslation.

The German poem has a very precise rhythm and rhyme:

Stäbe / hält / gäbe / Welt
Schritte / dreht / Mitte / steht
Pupille / hinein / Stille / zu sein

The English translations that keep to the rhyme scheme exactly have to mangle the language so thoroughly to get the rhymes to sound that we hear only that, and the poem disappears. Versions that try to keep to a strict equivalence in the English, for each word, lose their sense of being in the English language.

The version I have just read I cut out of a *New Yorker* magazine in 1984. It was the first time I had come across the poem, which felt for me, and I am sure for many others who read it for the first time, a revelation. I do not literally carry a copy folded in my wallet. But a photostat of the poem, from an article by George Steiner on Rilke, has been in my studio since 1984, together with newspaper cuttings, a photo of refugees in Burundi, a page from an encyclopedia, long since disemboweled, with the movement of the wings of a crane in flight; Chilembwe's letter, "The Voice of Africans in the Present War"; the last few pages of Mayakovsky's play *A Tragedy*—all collected in a file labeled IMPORTANT. NOT TO LOSE.

Since then I have read many different translations. But this first one I came across still seems to me the best. And there are many—enough to make a whole "Panther" translation convention. I could make an argument for each line, why

"it seems to him the world consists of bars and
railings, and beyond them the world exists no more."

is better than

"it seemed to him that thousands of bars are before him,
and behind them, nothing merely."

or,

"it seems to him there are a thousand bars
and behind the bars, no world."

The mid-line rhyme of

"it seems to him the world consists of bars and
railings, and beyond them the world exists no 'more.'"

The balance of "world consists" and "world exists" propels us into the rhythm of the walking—and so on, and so on.

The particularity of a private opinion always appears as an objective description of the world. This translation IS better. It is as if there is a Platonic judge, adjudicating objectively from his seat in the sun.

There is of course a close relationship to some of the words and the images: "welt" does mean "world." "Tanz" is a dance. But very soon, we are in a place where the marks shift. The "Vorhang der Pupille" is sometimes a curtain, a shutter, even a film. The "Tanz von kraft" is a "dance of strength," or a "ritual dance," or a "particular dance." This is the first level of dislocation. We are back at the anamorphic cylindrical mirror, making a distorted translation below on the paper, to see the original panther in the mirror above. The dislocation of the translation, the imperfect art of making a distorted mark, a new version on the paper below the mirror, so that its reflection in the mirror is similar to the German poem. In the mirror, you want to see

> Nur manchmal schiebt der
> Vorhang der Pupille
> sich lautlos auf—

as the poet writes; and on the sheet below, you try, "Just now and then the pupil's noiseless shutter is lifted"; "only sometimes when the pupil's film is soundlessly lifted"; or you try "yet at times, all noiseless, the pupil seems unveiled"; or "only sometimes does the shutter of his pupil's door slide open"; or "just sometimes lifts the curtains of his sensing, up soundlessly"; or "only at times the curtain of the pupil lifts quietly"; "only sometimes when the pupil's film soundlessly opens"; "yet from time to time the pupil's curtain rises silently." Some sound more euphonious than others. At times, the effort of translation seems to come too much to the front.

DEFENSIVE SLEEPING

But as with the anamorphic mirror, there is another level of transformation in the translation. The original poem is fixed. The translation has the double distance in the mirror. The shift and variations that different translators make, as in the way we alter the image by changing our relationship to the mirror, where it is always personal, always biographical.

I first saw the poem with the precise lines of the English version I read to you in 1984. It was as if those lines were being waited for. They were like advice that we only hear or heed when it corresponds to what we already know. The sense that the lines fit a space waiting for them. So one thinks, "How can a poet writing in Paris in 1902 have such a sense of who I am in Johannesburg in 1984?" A point of connection.

Rilke's poem has an anthropomorphism and reverse anthropomorphism. The panther does not so much become a person as a camera, and we become the shutter out of alignment, so all the film sees is the shutter. The world consists of the shutter, and behind the shutter, no world. The turning of the film reel, the pacing of the panther. And finally on film, the film-like image that gets past the shutter, traversing the reel of the film; it shudders through the tense stillness of the limbs to the heart and disappears. Into darkness, under-exposed; into a white blankness of over-exposure; but at any rate, an image held, and then lost. But this very anthropomorphism, or human machine-morphism, is there to bring us out of ourselves—to that part of us we don't know, the center we cannot grasp; the center where the will stands paralytically, the center where a mighty will was put to sleep.

What caught me when I read the poem in 1984 was not the description of the panther as a camera, as photographer, but the two lines:

> Like a dance of strength around a centre
> Where a mighty will was put to sleep.

They corresponded so closely to what it felt like to be in the studio. The urge to make something, a gathering of energy around . . . Around what? The blank page, the empty paper. An energy gathered, but not knowing what it should do. The impulse to make something, to draw or to paint something; but waiting for a clear instruction. What is to be done? What are the images to be made? As if the instruction would tell me: we are waiting to make a proletarian revolution. We are waiting to come out of the cave, into the sun. While the only thing I had confidence in was the very circling itself, the riddle that had no clear answer. The riddle that has a clear answer, necessarily, as every clear answer, an answer like "a man" to the riddle of the sphinx, always needs a sentry with a loaded rifle, a policeman, to protect the image, and also to keep it in order.

In the studio, this manifested itself in the split between an energy of tensing of muscles (sometimes this energy and impulse to work are located here, at the edge of the pectoral muscles, where we can almost taste the activity to come)—a split between this energy, and a lassitude, an inability to keep awake, that would sometimes come over. A defensive sleeping. An inability to know what should be made, or how to make, or why it should be made, masquerading as tiredness. A real tiredness, masking a fake tiredness. The need and not-need to make something. This is not an image I am burning to show, or story or experience I need to tell: this is the not-need; but the pressure for something to be there: the need.

Rilke wrote the poem "The Panther" when he was working as a secretary for the sculptor Auguste Rodin. He was stuck with the WHAT of writing: knowing he was a poet, and not knowing what the words should describe. Rodin sent him to the zoo, with the instruction not to come back until he had written about something he had seen. This is one of the great poems of the last century, and it started life as a homework exercise. But the relief in the poem is the relief of recognizing yourself. What had seemed a fault, a mistake, a moral weakness—this falling asleep at the job, the exhaustion that would come over me in the studio. I would look at what I had spent the morning drawing—and then sit down on a chair at the back of the studio to get a larger view; and then close one eye and squint at it, then the other eye, trying through an act of will to improve what I saw.

Then closing both eyes, and drifting off with the mantra, "Let this time pass. Let this time pass."

But reading the poem, this fault was passed back into the world: this is how it is. This is what we see in "The Panther," this split between energy, possibility—and the gap. The sleep in the body, or the blank paper in the studio, and then the writing of the poem. The making of the drawings, filling the studio with them, their presence on the walls a record of the dance around the center.

The magnet of the poem—that it should stay in the studio for these twenty-seven years: partly connecting to the charcoal blackness of the panther, meeting the thought of drawing half-way: a panther. God in the charcoal dust. The pacing, and the gap. The meeting on the paper, the membrane between what is us, and what is outside of us, what we can comprehend, and the animal unconscious, unknowingness that sits inside of us. Here is not just a distant sending of signals from the outside world to us, but something that pulls the two together.

The panther in Paris, the studio in Johannesburg, meeting on the page. The panther changed to words, to meet the projection from the outside world that is waiting for it—for the mix of energy, the certainty of desire, and the radical hollow at the center of it.

END DRAWING LESSON FIVE

Drawing Lesson Six

ANTI-ENTROPY

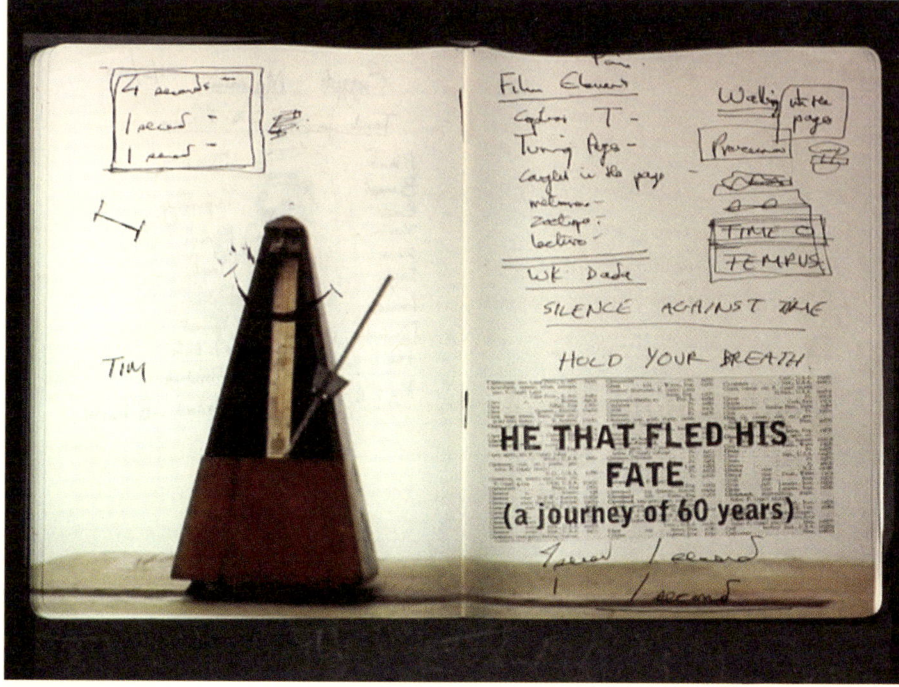

Film Elements
TIME
TEMPUS
SILENCE AGAINST
HOLD YOUR BREATH
TIM
HE THAT FLED HIS
FATE
(a journey of 60 years)

NOSTOS 1: HE THAT FLED HIS FATE

When I was eight years old, my father took me and my sister on a train journey from Johannesburg to Port Elizabeth. On the train he read us the story of Perseus and the slaying of the Gorgon Medusa, from a book of children's stories of Greek myths.

King Acrisius of Argos asked the Oracle how long he would live. The Oracle declined to give him a number, but told him he would be killed by his grandson. King Acrisius, terrified, had his own daughter Danae locked in a chamber with neither door nor window. But Zeus, king of the gods, saw her through a crack in the wall. He entered the room as a shower of gold. He seduced and impregnated Danae. I am not sure how my father dealt with this part of the story for an eight-year-old. But Danae bears a son, Perseus, and King Acrisius, enraged, terrified, has Danae and the infant Perseus placed in a wooden chest and has the chest thrown into the sea.

But instead of sinking, the chest with its two inmates washes up on the shore of the Island of Seriphos, where the shepherd Dictys finds it. The shepherd looks after Danae and her son; and in due course Perseus grows into a muscular, agile youth. He is, after all, the son of a god. Meanwhile, the King of Seriphos, Polydectes, has heard of the beauty of Danae and wants her as his concubine. But fearing the protective wrath of her son Perseus, he sends Perseus on a suicidal mission. Perseus is sent to kill the Gorgon Medusa—and this is the heart of the myth. The Gorgons are a tribe of women too terrifying to behold. Their hair is made of living snakes, and to look at them is to turn to stone.

NOT TO BE LOOKED AT

The page of the book with the drawing of Medusa was to be turned quickly, to be glimpsed but not looked at. It fell into a category of images too powerful to contemplate. One could add to that list:

> the red, enraged, terrifying head of Beethoven, in Percy Scholes's *Oxford Companion to Music;*
> the image of the Loathly Lady from a children's telling of Chaucer's *Canterbury Tales;*
> the fire that cannot be looked at by the prisoners in the cave;
> the sun that cannot be looked at by the prisoners when they emerge from the cave into the sunlight.

To get back to Perseus: He sets out on his journey. The gods help him. He is given wings on his shoes to make him swift. He is given a cloak of invisibility. And he is given a reflective shield, so that instead of having to look at Medusa directly, he can look at her reflection in the shield—the curved shield an anamorphic mirror giving him a safe translation of Medusa—and avoid being turned to stone. He uses these aids, and with his demigod's power, he slays Medusa. He binds her head to his shield, and he starts his return.

Perseus, who has been told of the Oracle's prediction, decides to return to his ancestral island, the island of his grandfather, the aged King Acrisius, to show him he bears him no ill will, has no desire to kill him. All has turned out well in the end. All he desires is to make peace with him.

But meanwhile news has traveled to Argos that Perseus has slain the Gorgon Medusa, and that Perseus is on his way to Argos. King Acrisius immediately thinks of the Oracle and knows that Perseus is on his way to kill him. So King Acrisius flees his kingdom and his island, disguised as a beggar in sackcloth and ashes.

Perseus is approaching the island of Argos but decides to stop off at the nearby island of Larissa, to take part in an athletics contest being held there. He has killed a Gorgon, he is half god, he has high hopes of success in the games—and says that if he wins the laurel wreath he will take this as a gift to his grandfather. He takes part in the discus competition. The stands are crowded; there is expectation in the air.

Perseus takes the stone discus in his left hand. He builds up momentum, rocking backward and forward, his body undulating as the strength in him grows. He transfers the discus to his right hand, leans back, and launches it. It sails over the grassy field, past the marks of the other competitors. The discus soars over the edge of the field and into the stands. In the last row of spectators it strikes an old man, a beggar, in sackcloth and ashes—and kills him.

For me this was intolerable. If only the grandfather had not sat in that seat. Why not one seat to the left, or one seat to the right? He would have been safe. Why did Perseus have to take part in the athletics competition? Why did he have to show off? Why did the grandfather have to run away? How could so many chance events, so many unlikely elements—the discus, the disguise, the date of the athletics competition—how could all of these conspire to make the predicted inevitability? Maybe every step I took, or didn't take, was the wrong one. Maybe every decision, which seemed so unimportant, would lead to consequences so much greater. Every decision was the wrong decision. If Perseus or his grandfather had just read the last page of the book, this could all have been avoided. But once launched, the discus could not be called back.

This story of Perseus is a *nostos*, a poem of return. All Perseus's adventures are episodes in the course of his return to his home. The arc of the discus completes the nostos. The discus is launched at birth; we await its return. The most familiar nostos, of course, is Homer's *Iliad* and *The Odyssey*, the story of Ulysses, who sets out for the Trojan war, spends ten years in

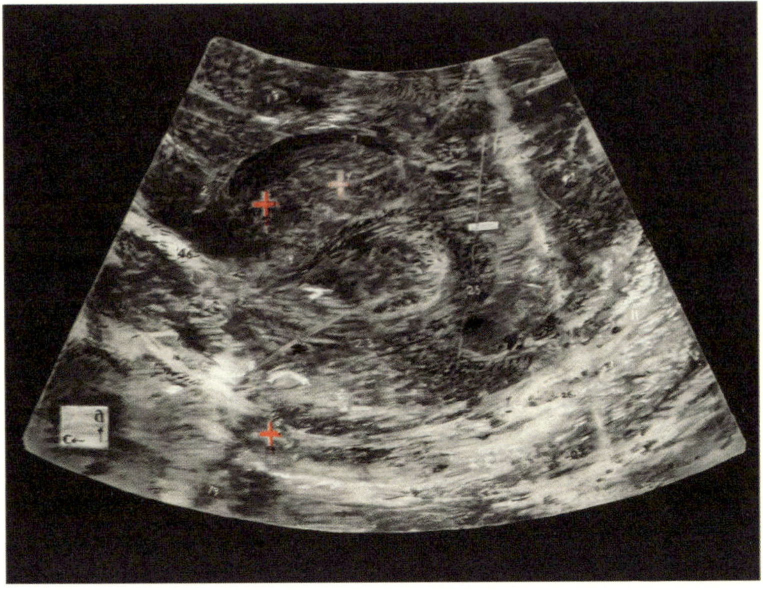

the war, and then ten years returning to his island of Ithaca, to reclaim Penelope from her suitors.

L'HUMANA FRAGILITA

Some years ago I directed a production of Monteverdi's opera *Il Ritorno di Ulisse in Patria*. One of the questions we had to solve in the production was the relationship of Ulysses to fortune, to Fate. Ulysses is up against the gods who govern the sea, the storms, who erect or remove the obstacles he faces on his journey home. The gods are forces beyond ourselves. We are at the mercy of their rages and their whims, knowing that all efforts, acts, creations are made in their shadow. In *Ulisse,* it is the gods who release thunderbolts and storms. Nowadays thunderbolts are less terrifying; we can put up lightning protectors. But there are still things that exact the same terror.

We do not have a fear anymore of the external lightning stroke. But we have the terror of the internal lightning bolt, of the heart attack, of the stroke, of the body betraying us. So although we do not make libations to the gods and go to burn incense in the temple, the way we used to, we do this in our own ways: forswearing smoking, giving up fatty foods, going to the temple of the gym. Trying to appease that part of us that on the one hand is separate from us, but that on the other hand we know at some point is going to betray us and kill us. The lightning bolts of fate, unleashed by the gods against Ulysses, now become internal lightning bolts, a lightning strike of dye around the blood vessels of the heart.

The split and separation between that part of ourselves of which we are conscious and have control, and that other self, the insides of our body. That dark inner self we take for granted, a body moving in parallel to our conscious selves. A dark, wet unknown we hope will pump, digest, move for us. That sends messages on to us, with whom we live in better or worse accord. The cave we know through X-rays, scans, other probings, knowing that what is growing inside us is not just our lives.

We are caught between the internal clock of our heart and the inescapable arc of the discus. There are displacements here. First the shift from the external constraining forces and fate, to the inside of the body. The power of the gods brought inside, to what is still invisible, but which we know is both of us and beyond our control.

A second displacement. This internal imaging, this internal split—at simplest, between our skin and that which is underneath it—obviously refers to that other gap within ourselves: the gap between who we are, and all the other possible selves we sense but cannot reach. Where we are at the brink of an understanding but are shut out by a phrase that keeps repeating again and again in our head: "The 15cm circuit of the brain. The 15cm circuit of the brain. The 15cm circuit of the brain. The 15cm circuit of the brain."

Here the physical, the dye around the heart, the MRI scan, becomes a way of envisioning more invisible other selves and othernesses.

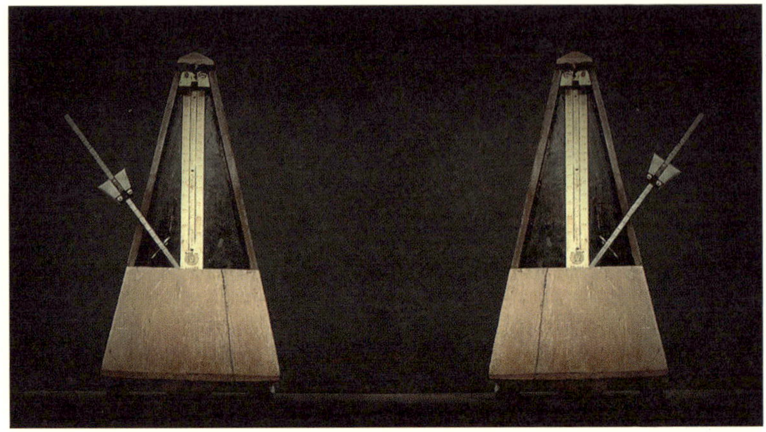

The idea I almost had disappears like a dream we are trying to carry from the depths of sleep up to wakefulness, only to let it slip as we reach the surface. We try to grab the image as it recedes.

We take the external world, bring it inside us to understand who we are, and then project it out and beyond, against the dye in the heart, against the arc of the discus.

We are at the final lecture, and we return home here. All the other lectures have taken as their Ur-text some images or some reference to work that I have made in the past. Perhaps it is appropriate for the final lecture to have as its referent a work that is still in progress—that will be completed in the next two months. At one point I hoped that this project would become these six lectures. That did not work. Then I hoped the lectures would be the basis for the performance and installation; and we have the uneven resolution here, somewhere between a text and a drawing of a clock.

Over the last year, while writing these lectures, I have been working on a project called *The Refusal of Time*—a messy, overlapping series of films, dances, drawings. The project bifurcated and became an installation, *The Refusal of Time*, and a performance, *Refuse the Hour*. The performance consisted of a lecture broken into seven sections, five of which are included in this

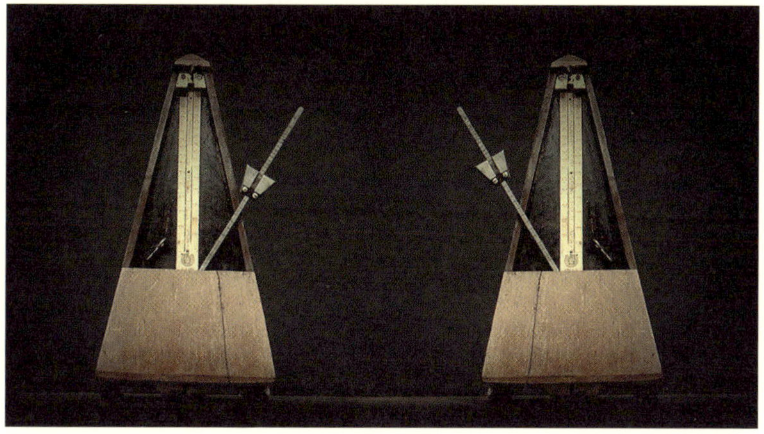

sixth Norton lecture. A dancer, four singers, seven musicians were on stage for the lecture.

Time is not a new subject to introduce at this stage of the lectures. We have been tracking time and its transformations throughout the series. In the first lecture we looked at time turned to celestial distance, positing space as a universal archive of images we could recapture if we could be at the right distance from the source of their generation (Jupiter, where the start of this lecture is passing).

In Lecture Two, we were concerned among other things with the contraction and expansion of operatic time. Subjective time, a moment of thought expanded into the four minutes of an aria.

Geological time was a theme in Lecture Three, the two-billion-year history of Johannesburg and its meteor impact. Time turned into human history and metallurgy.

In Lecture Four time turned into the material of studio distance. The one-and-a-half-second sweep of the arm transformed into thirty-five two centimeter divisions of a line waiting for drawing and erasure. Time held in the paper and a roll of film.

In Lecture Five time is trapped in the zoetrope. An action moving forward but held in the same place.

The project *The Refusal of Time* began with considerations

of different kinds of time, but as the work progressed it became clear that it was as much about Fate as about Time; and our attempts to escape from that which insists on what and how and where we are. But there was more than that. There was a hope that if I started with the practical activities of design of sets, costumes, musical instruments, machinery, the direction and thrust of the lectures could be changed to a path I had not taken before—as if I could change not just their trajectory but their final destination.

PNEUMATIC TIME

We have spent much time in the nineteenth century talking about fixing time in the form of photography, looking at time running backward in early cinema, at attempts to capture and codify the speed of light, at the attempts to put a European constriction and control over the rest of the globe, in the form of nineteenth-century colonialism—all attempts to wrest control of the world and bring it to order.

In the nineteenth century in Paris, there was an attempt to bring time to order. A network of pipes and tubes was constructed under the streets of Paris, with the idea of bringing hygienic time to institutions and citizens of the city.

[Five musicians from Harvard play a variation of music by Philip Miller for *Refuse the Hour*. They remain on stage for the rest of the lecture.]

A mother clock was made with a powerful bellows, and every minute the mother clock would give a pant of air, a breath, which would travel down the thick pipes in the grand boulevards, be distributed into thinner pipes in the smaller streets, and divided further into narrow tubes that led to the municipal offices, train stations, and private subscribers, who would receive this officially approved breath of air in their daughter clocks. Every minute the clocks would all shift one minute. Breathe, wait a minute, breathe, wait a minute, breathe . . . A whole city breathing in unison, regulating themselves to the mistress clock, which stood in for the idea of perfect time, of perfect order.

Here we have a meeting of the clock as body, and the body as clock, as if one way of comprehending the world is to take all its attributes and all its elements and map them onto our body, into who we are. As if in our very breathing we are both enacting and able to resist time. If we could know the number of breaths in our lives, the 490 million, the 530 million breaths we will take, and then—breathe more slowly, hold our breath—in our very bodies resisting time coming toward us. Knowing we will run out of breaths, knowing we will always sit in the wrong seat. And knowing the discus will hit us, wherever we sit—but unable to stop ourselves from changing chairs as if our lives depended on it. At the very least, trying to make the journey of the discus broken by unexpected arabesques. But holding our breath against time.

TIME AS GEOGRAPHY

Time can be turned into distance, and through this, time becomes geography. The nineteenth-century coordination of clocks was undertaken to synchronize the clocks with stations in Europe. The cities of Europe would no longer construct their individual noons from when the sun was at its zenith. Basel and Paris would no longer have noon seven minutes apart, but would sacrifice their own noon for the sake of commerce and coordinated agreement.

The perfection of chronometers had long been the aim of geographers, to fix more precisely the positions of islands and continents in relation to Europe. With the spread of cables under sea and over land that followed the development of electronic telegraphy, time was taken from the master clocks of London and Paris and sent to the colonies.

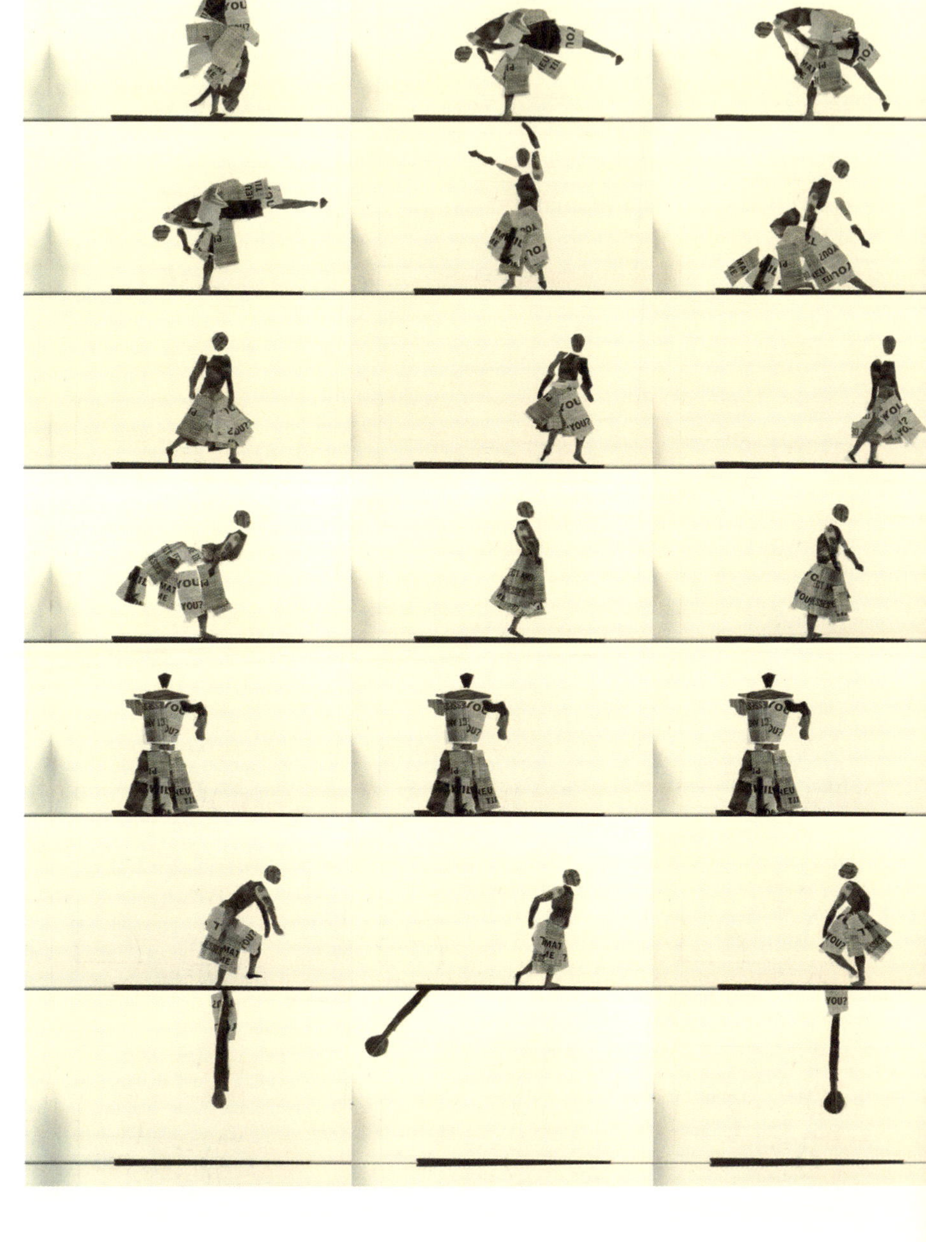
YOU?

Strings of cables, birds' nests of copper, turned the world into a giant switchboard, for commerce and control. The world was covered by a huge dented bird cage of time zones, of lines of agreement of control, all sent out by the clock rooms of Europe.

The lines on maps were miniature renderings of the real lines of cables that snaked around continents, or drew great arcs across the floors of the oceans. Sending and receiving stations followed the cable and marked the end of lines tethering the center to the satellite colony. The clock and the colonial observatory completed the mapping of the world.

The resistance to colonial rule—the Chilembwe revolt of 1915, the Herero revolt of 1906, the movement and actions against Europe, that spread through all the continents and colonies, while articulated in terms of cattle and land, were all attempts to resist the weight and control of Europe. GIVE US BACK OUR SUN. As if blowing up a train line could blow up the pendulum of the European clock, which swung over every head.

ANTI-ENTROPY

Let us look at what this resistance means. The universal certainty showing its cracks. A resistance to the dictates arriving from the center: a calibration of the cracks and fragmentations.

Entropy, as we are all familiar, talks about the degree of disorder or randomness within a system. Entropy is a measure of the unavailability, in a system, of the thermal energy of that system to be converted into work. It can be most easily described as a tendency for order to dissolve into disorder. It refers to the breakdown of something that leaves its site of generation as a coherent thought, a coherent object, a coherent image—and gradually disintegrates, becomes fragmentary; so that when it reaches its site of reception, what arrives are shards and fragments.

CONCERNING ENTROPY

Concerning Entropy no. 1

Take a vase. Use a no. 9 hammer and rap firmly on the rim. Smash the thing. All the pieces, with their half-athletes, the discus, the tree, the maiden—all in pieces. Place shards in a hat. Shake vigorously. Spread the evidence. Read your fortune.

Concerning Entropy no. 2

[In the performance *Refuse the Hour*, "Concerning Entropy no. 2" is accompanied by a solo violin. In "Concerning Entropy no. 3" a second voice joins the violin. In "Concerning Entropy no. 4" and "Concerning Entropy no. 5," a trumpet, tuba, and percussion are added to the ensemble.]

Take the vase. Use a no. 9 hammer and rap firmly on the rim.
Smash the thing. All the pieces with half-athletes,
the discus,
the tree,
the maiden,
the king,
the grandfather,
the oracle,
the fisherman,
the shield,
the sandals,
the cloak,
the shower of gold,
the right chair,
the wrong chair,
the wrong chair,
the wrong chair,
the wrong chair,

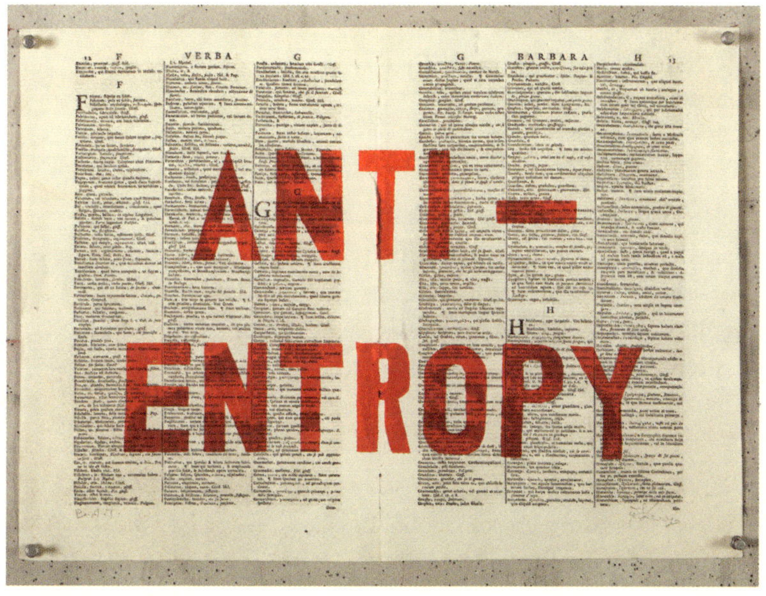

the chains,
the Gorgon,
the sun—
. . . all in pieces.
Place shards in a hat. Shake vigorously. Spread the evidence.
Read your fortune.

Concerning Entropy no. 3

The evidence with Place.
Take a firmly maiden
Stir vigorously the shards, fragmented and read.
Athletes,
a hat,
no. 9 on the shards

All spread
rap
rim

smash
use
Hammer your vase fortune.
A discus thing.
All.

Concerning Entropy no. 4

Hammer on the shards
maidens firmly all
With tap discus
Place, use,
Fragmented.
edge all thing.
A hat your fortune
smash
Shards in stir
The evidence? A vase.
Read Spread vigorously
No. 9 Athletes
  Take a . . . and . . .

Concerning Entropy no. 5

rap maidens With athletes your read

Place on the discus
Spread rim

The telegraph
The breathing lung
The beating clock
The reel of string
The directory
The atlas
The encyclopedia

The donkey
The prisoners in the cave
The collapse of the drive-in cinema
The letter to the newspaper unpublished
The Bushman family preparing their meal, in the storeroom of the museum
The *Vernichtungsbefehl*
All the translations of "The Panther" waiting in line
The two rhinoceri: the rhinoceros of the right eye, the rhinoceros of the left eye
Waiting for the right barrel
Waiting for the left barrel

the horizon
the perpendicular
the acute
the arcane
the reflex

The shards in a hat
and fragmented thing
Use all fortune
Smash . . .

What is the hope? That through the course of the last five lectures, there are images or thoughts that have remained, even in fragmented form. The invitation is to try to hold onto a narrative, or to construct a narrative; to prevent the different elements from disappearing into an even state of disorder and background radiation.

In the lecture here, a note:
WAIT FOR THE FOG IN YOUR HEAD TO LIFT

This won't happen; we will have to continue.

Let us trace our journey, its geography.
In Lecture One we started underground, in the cave of Plato.
In Lecture Two we narrowed our investigation to the Enlightenment, and the colonies, particularly Africa.
In Lecture Three we moved the focus to the city of Johannesburg.
In Lecture Four we zoned in on the studio.
Last week we closed in on the bookshelf in the poem "The Panther," by Rilke.
Today we continue the investigation, pinned to the eye of the needle: two lines from Rilke's poem.

At the end of the last lecture, we left off with Rilke's poem "The Panther," and in particular the lines describing the panther's walk around his cage as "a dance of strength around a centre where a mighty will was put to sleep." There is no avoiding it. On the one hand, it is the circle in the studio, the endless walking around the studio, with phrases going through one's head, repeating endlessly, hat, typewriter, tool chest; hat, typewriter, tool chest; tool chest, typewriter, hat; panther . . . Trying to stop the stupid, limited words that keep on arriving, endlessly, the same phrases, the same words. On the one hand hoping the walk itself will produce new words, on the other hand the walk itself lulling the words into a familiar and over-familiar pattern.

The circle is also the zoetrope, the action that continuously returns to where it began, and repeats itself. Again, pushing an expectation never realized, that the image will escape the zoetrope and take us to some new land. It becomes a *nostos* on a small scale, the panther circling in his cage; the one end of the cage four meters away, his Troy, the feeding bowl at the other side of the cage his Ithaca, to which he returns. Only to set out again: Ithaca, Troy, Ithaca, Troy . . .

But to get to the center itself. To approach from a different angle. How or why does one become an artist? Again here we go back to Rilke's panther, and to the radical insufficiency, the radical gap in the center. There has to be some gap, some lack,

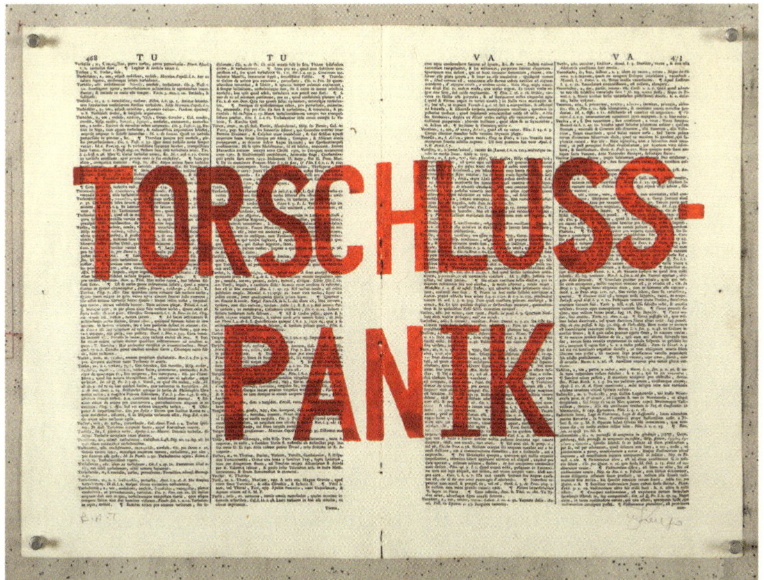

which provokes people to spend 20 years, 30 years, making drawings, leaving tracings of themselves. It has to do with the need to see oneself in other people's looking at what you have made. An insufficiency in the self, the need to be a snail, leaving a trail of yourself as you move through the world. Hansel, leaving a trail of crumbs to lead you home.

To leave a report of the journey around the center on the walls of the studio, of galleries, of museums. As if it is in the reflection of people looking at these traces that one finds one's existence.

TORSCHLUSSPANIK

Can we escape who we are?

I think of myself as an artist making drawings, even when the charcoal is replaced by an ink word. Being led by a line, in this case a line of ink or a pen. A kind of lapidary thinking or drawing, an embroidery of thought to bring us to some new sentence or image (and then take this back). Even as each word of the lecture is said, it cuts off the possibility of all the other thoughts. The barrel of the pen refilled with the words absorbed. The pen a loaded weapon.

Can a drawing escape where it is going?

[Show video projection of images formed by falling flakes of black paper. The images are displaced by a breath, and then settle down on the page as another image.]

When one is circling the studio, about to begin, all is possible. But as it lands, all that potential becomes . . . a coffee pot. Launched again, a new sheet of paper, the possibilities there; only for it to be . . . another coffee pot. Can you be better than you are?

There is the hope for something new, but what arrives? A typewriter. Trying for something and what will arrive? . . . another coffee pot. A rhinoceros. We are reduced to making a self-portrait as a coffee pot, a rhinoceros, a typewriter, a megaphone. A new sheet of paper. All the energy waiting in the arm, gathering for its decision. While the shards are in the air, there is the possibility of . . . of . . . of . . .

That this time, THIS TIME IT WILL BE DIFFERENT.

All that we wish we could be. And there is the *torschlusspanik*, the fear that with decision, each final arrival of the image, all the other images are cut out, the door to other possibilities closes behind us, and we turn in panic to the sound of that closing door.

What would we wish?

For the shards to land, for once, as a phrase in the subjunctive, in French ultramarine?
A diagram of a galaxy, in cobalt violet?

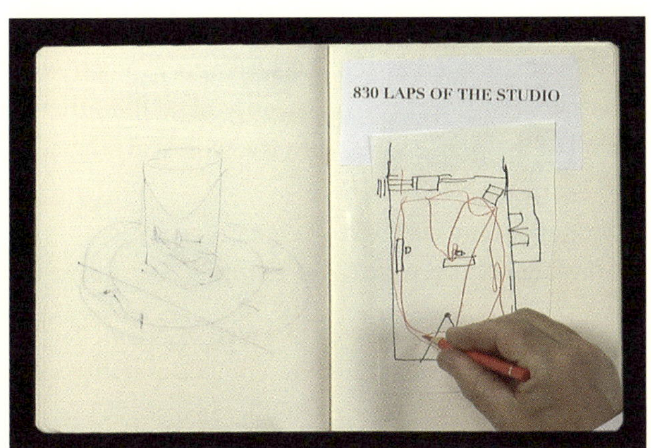
830 LAPS OF THE STUDIO

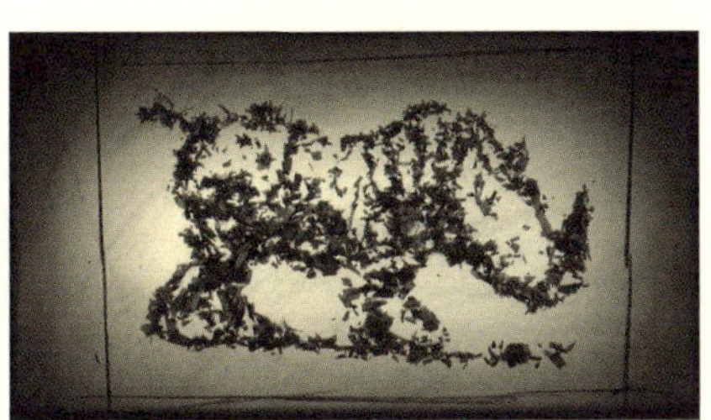

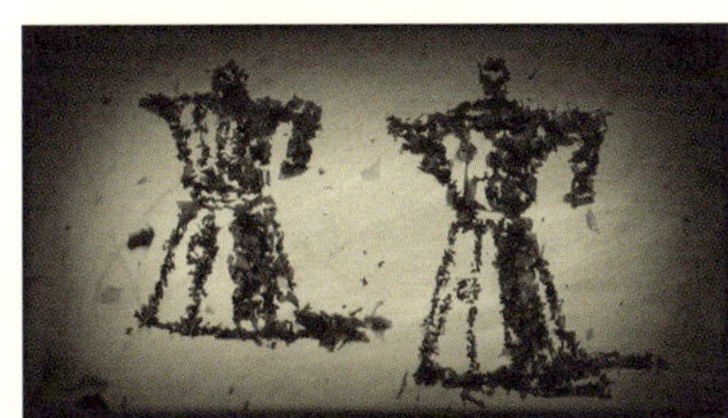

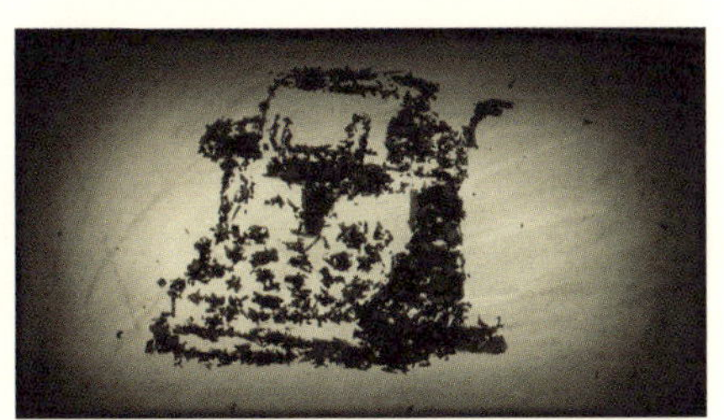

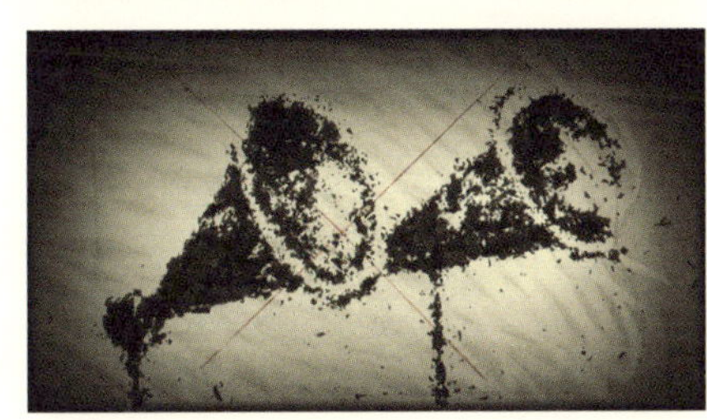

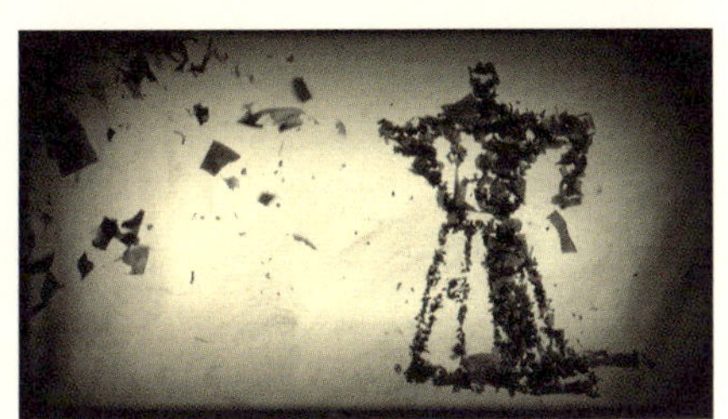

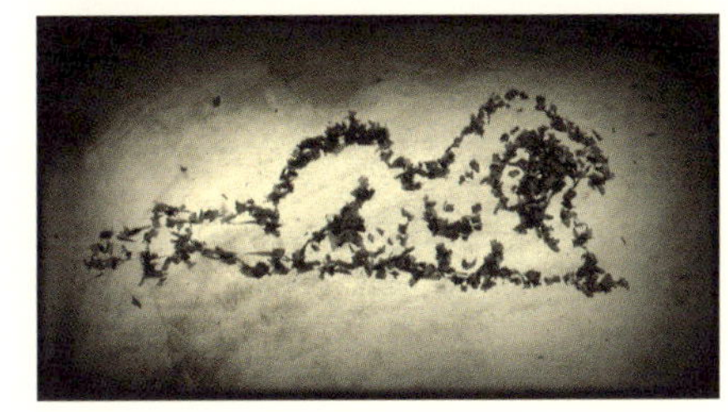

A gryphon—a baby sphinx in one's arms?
A clear line of sight, from slavery and Greek society to the center of the convolutions of the present political crises?
A painting of peonies by Robert Motherwell, in rose madder alizarin?
The design of a new escapement for a watch?
For once, just one unguarded, unqualified declarative certainty?
Even as these ideas emerge, they become so limited, and so small, and the gap between what we are and that which part of us feels we are or could be, gets larger and larger; and the only safe space is on the margins of that circle.

ROOM OF FAILURES

I have a pile of notebooks—lectures begun and abandoned.

The lectures themselves took their own direction. I would have liked to have talked about many different things. I made notes for a lecture about Titian, and the painting of Danae in the Shower of Gold. I found many interesting comments by Michelangelo about correct painting and the poor work being done by his contemporaries.

Another lecture was going to deal with the erotics of looking, going from Titian, the glimpse, seeing and not seeing, looking and not looking. About a surfeit of looking, when a fixed gaze held for too long can turn desire to ashes—or at any rate to a contemplation of pigment, canvas, varnish.

There was a third lecture containing interesting observations on Perseus's story, of Atlas with the world on his shoulders. But these failed, they stopped, and we follow the path that we have taken.

There was a lecture on Gandhi and Kojeve and the master-slave dialectic. And the ethics of reconciliation. A beautiful lecture, but written by a friend, not me.

I tried to keep away from the studio, to NOT talk about my work, to talk only about other people's work. But I failed. The lectures arrived, saying: this is who you are, and this is all that you are, and you shall not escape.

NOSTOS 4

A Ghanaian proverb:

He that fled his fate, a journey of sixty years,
While he was going it waited for him—seated next to the gutter side:
And it said, "Come let us eat,—my dear friend!"
And when he asked it, "Who is it?"—it said, "Am I not thy fate?"

NOSTOS 14: TWINS

The Ghanaian aphorism is retold in 1905 by Einstein. One twin brother stands on a platform of a train station, and he ages more quickly than his twin brother in a carriage passing through the station. Their clocks, synchronized at birth, are out of kilter. A new accommodation has to be made between them. Take a larger journey. One twin sets out for a journey in space, and one stays behind. They wave to each other. Together, their waves are coordinated. But then offset by the sending and receiving of waves. The traveling brother's wave gets larger and slower. His hand is hardly moving—the unmoving upraised hand pushes the brother away. While to the traveling brother, his brother on the shore is more and more agitated; his waving arm oscillates faster and faster, until the farewell gesture becomes a vibrating fist.

The traveling twin has a journey of 20 years. But so much happens on his journey: adventures with Gorgons, with Atlas carrying the world on his shoulder, with sirens, with witches—that the 20 years he is away seem a lifetime. For the twin staying at home, the days are the same, and the years that pass disappear into their sameness, so that the 60, 80, 200 years he waits for his brother feel the same time, no time, and an eternity.

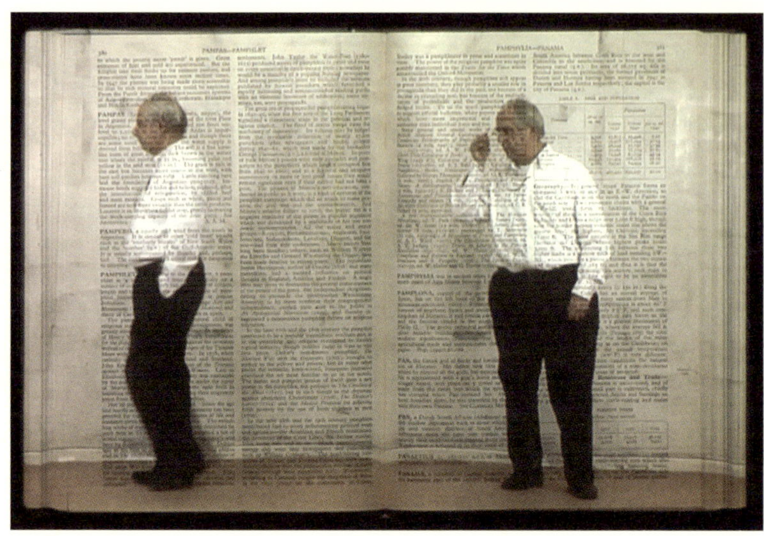

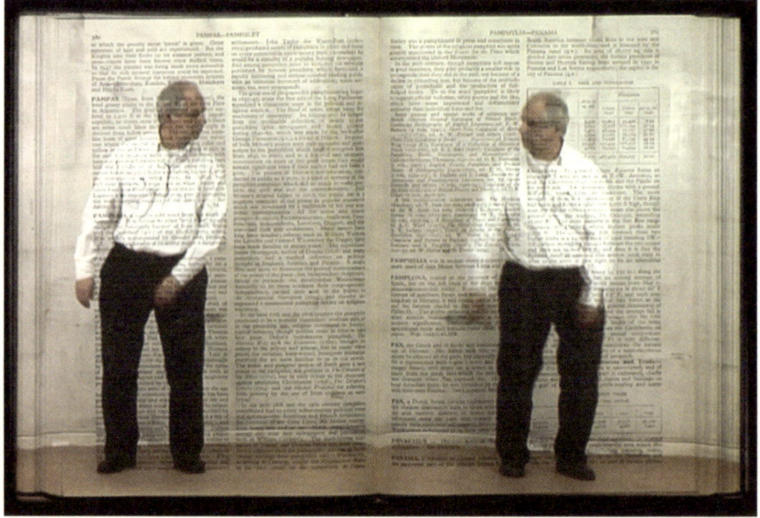

And when the messenger comes to say, "We must celebrate, for he who has voyaged has returned"—the one at home, now so aged, can only look up and say, "Who?"

This split of twins we have observed at different points in these lectures, in the gap between the abilities of the self and the shadow of the self, the speed, the agility, the dexterity, of one's own shadow—it is of me but more than me. In the split between the artist as maker, and the artist as viewer.

I am aware of other twins. The self in Johannesburg, writing these notes, projecting myself into Harvard. Myself here, in Harvard now, thinking back and cursing his self in Johannesburg for not having got it right, for not having written better notes, leaving me high and dry.

[Show projection of William Kentridge in the Johannesburg studio, talking to the audience or looking to the side to William Kentridge delivering the lecture in Harvard. Johannesburg-self words are heard as audio recording, Harvard-self words are spoken live.]

The Johannesburg self:

Do not complain. The notes are sufficient. It is up to you to use them well.

TELEGRAPH MESSAGES BETWEEN THE TWO

The Harvard self:

All the possible things you could have written about, all the possible things I could have been speaking about, reduced here to this contemplation of self.

The Johannesburg self:

What do you need? Big statements? Answers to universal questions? The artist reveals mystic truths?

The Harvard self:

You could at least have written about the responsibilities of the artist, the duties of the artist, the obligations of the artist.

Johannesburg self:

The duties of the artist?

TURN PAGES OF BOOK

Johannesburg self:

I have it here, under *Duties of the Artist:*

Put fresh water in the dog bowl.
Work.

Harvard self:
Work?

The Johannesburg self:
No, "WORK" crossed out, "PLAY." "WORK" crossed out. "WORK" crossed out, "PLAY." "Sleep."
The artist is at work EVEN when he is sleeping.

Harvard artist to the audience:
Such wide ambition reduced to this. He has not said a word about Clement Greenberg and his visit to Johannesburg in 1975.

Johannesburg self:
I have written about what happens in the studio.

Harvard self:
You haven't said a word about art in the era of multiple biennales.

Johannesburg self:
I have written about what happens in the studio.

Harvard self:
You have not once mentioned Mr. Derrida, Mr. Foucault.

Johannesburg self:
We did refer to G. W. F. Hegel. John Rawls and Franz Fanon were in Lecture Two, but they left after the second draft.

Harvard self:
Do you really think there is no place for intellectuals in the studio?

Johannesburg self:
I am not saying that. They should be invited for coffee. But generally, while the work is happening, they are better on the bench outside the door.

Harvard self:
You take your chances with that answer. In this space.

Johannesburg self:
Am I correct when I say we are back where we started? Using a Socratic method of question and answer?

Harvard self:

I had not noted it, but that is so. Inevitably so.

Johannesburg self:

Is the Socratic method not appropriate to Harvard University?

Harvard self:

Let's not go down that road.

Johannesburg self:

There are three more pages of notes and dialogue that continue here . . .

Harvard self:

Basta! Enough! We have had stupidity as a theme for far too many of these lectures. Can we not change how you go?

Johannesburg self:

All right. I write the note in Johannesburg:

STOP WRITING. At 2:10 pm on the 25th of February, 2012.

You have five minutes on your own to say what you like, make it up, improvise, before we get to the concluding section of these lectures. Patience, Ithaca is in sight.

[WK still. Long silence.]

It seemed a good idea at the time.

[Long pause.]

Four and a half minutes to go. Four minutes and thirty-three seconds.

[Long pause.]

Five is the loop and the space between the loop. Final and the absence of final.

Sense is the words and the gap between the words.

[Pause.]

Too many words.

[Pause.]

I should have said more to my father, have spoken more to him, placed as he is in the center of the cage.

The Johannesburg self *(whistle, fingers in mouth):*

If I may interrupt. There was a section here that I meant to put in. That we forgot. A section about collisions, about particular collisions, before we reach the black hole at the end. About the artist running around the studio, the other self running in the opposite direction, until we get a collision. We were talking about Ulysses, I mean we have to bring in Tennyson:

Harvard self:

"It little profits that an idle king . . .

Though much is taken, much abides . . ."

Johannesburg self:

We can do a collision between Alfred, Lord Tennyson and Samuel Beckett:

Harvard self:

"To strive. To find."

Johannesburg self:

"To fail. To fail better . . ."

Johannesburg self:

". . . and not to yield."

Harvard self:

". . . and not to yield."

Johannesburg self:

—I didn't want us to forget that. All right. You still have another 2 minutes. See what can be rescued.

Harvard self:

Do I believe in these lectures?

[Pause.]

I think each time I have convinced myself I have mistrusted the conviction. I wanted the lectures to be a demonstration rather than an argument. A demonstration in a lecture theater of what happens in the studio. Using language, rhetorical devices, as one would use paper and charcoal and glue to construct an object (a drawing or a lecture) that embodies a will toward meaning. Even if that meaning is about the elusiveness, the uncertainty, of the project itself.

Johannesburg self:
30 seconds . . .

10 seconds . . .

THE FULL STOP SWALLOWS THE SENTENCE

These twins refer back, of course, to the stereoscope we described in Lecture Four, the double image, left eye, right eye, that we construct into a coherent illusion of stability and coherence in space.

This is what the artist does. Takes the fragments, the shards, and rearranges them. From the broken bicycle, handle bars and saddle, he makes a bull. He tries to distract the inconsolable child. "Here. Look at this. With our hands we can make a shadow on the wall. An old woman, a bird, a horse."

This is the artist's project: needing the fragments, even delighting in them, in the project of wresting meaning from them.

The meaning is always a construction, a projection, not an edifice—something to be made, not simply found. There is always a radical incoherence and a radical instability. All certainties can only be held together by a text, a threat, an army, a fatwa, a sermon—that holds the fragments in an iron grip.

We return to the beginning, ready to enter the cave, this time carrying the rusted bicycle frame, the box of broken pottery, the bones of the last rhinoceros. Ready to take our place in the procession, to throw our shadows onto the wall of the cave. We come to the dark center of the panther's circle.

When mass is huge, gravity grows until it is irresistible. A black hole traps all that passes, allowing out of its gravitational field no object, no light, no trace of light that has been attracted

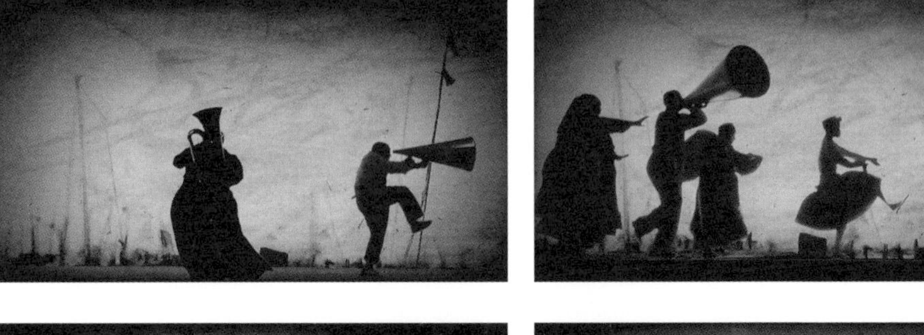
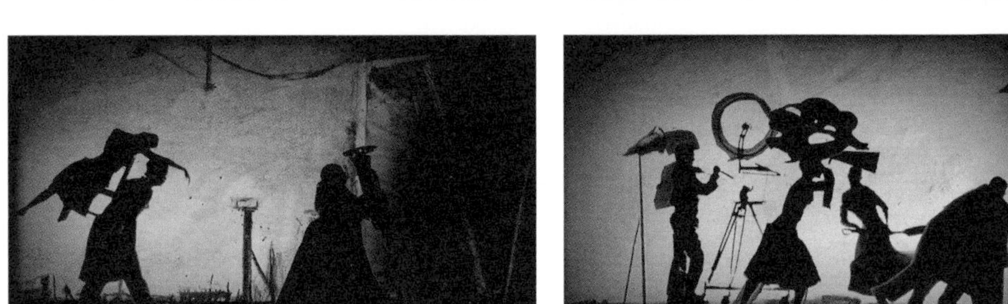
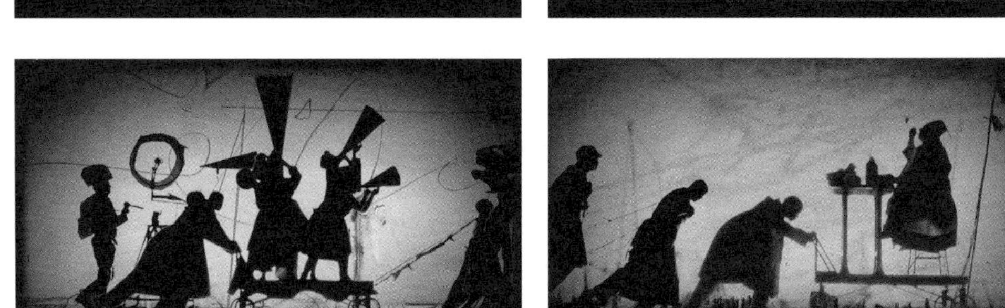
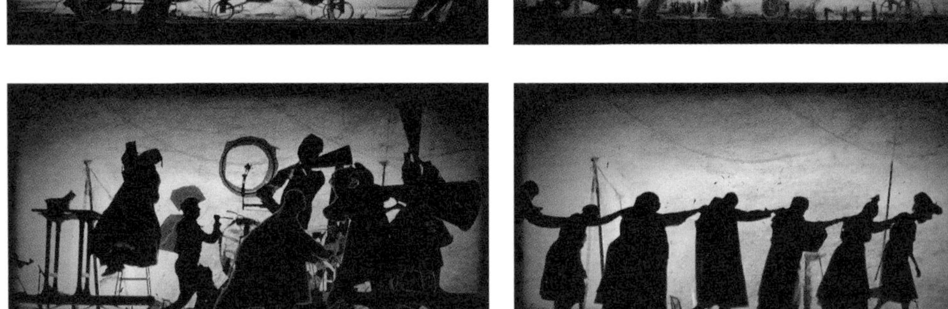

to it. A black hole the size of a full stop swallows the sentence. Others swallow a house, a city, a galaxy. The journey of the projection of an image comes to an end. Perseus, Danae, the grandfather, the zoetrope, the bellows in the clock room in Paris, the eight-year-old on a train journey with his father, all the volumes of the library, are swallowed by the black hole.

[Projection of procession of figures carrying objects. The stage band plays. The projected images are the penultimate images of the projections in *The Refusal of Time* and *Refuse the Hour*.]

Is all gone, none to be retrieved? Entropy forbids all elements from entering the black chasm. As an object approaches a black hole, its wavelength lengthens, slowing down, becomes redder and redder; the information and attributes separate from the object and remain as strings—vibrating strings, twists, knots, cat's cradles of information, vibrating and circling the edge of the event horizon. The bank at the edge of the River Styx, where Charon deposits those headed for the black darkness of Hades. He keeps in his boat the attributes they have shed. A suitcase of teeth, a pile of shoes, a sheaf of words, an old stone discus. Held in trust on account, waiting to be decoded, for the shards to be rearranged, to be made new.

END DRAWING LESSON SIX